*Are
You
Planning*

VOLUME I

Are You Planning

☐ A wedding?

☐ A future divorce?

☑ A healthy marriage?

25 Lessons Learned from my First Twenty-five Years

Stacey Prater-White

This book is dedicated to my "A-Team" and my tribe of nieces and nephews. I'm counting on you all to show the next generation how wonderful marriage is.

Love,
Mom
Aunna Stace

Table of Contents

Acknowledgements

Rozelle Fredrick White Jr., words fail me...thank you for saying "I do" every day in word and deed. I have witnessed the work you do to become "The Total Package" and God is pleased. Never give up, Babe.

Amber, Andrew and Austin; there aren't words to adequately describe my borderline illegal obsession with you three. My daily conversation with the Lord is that He gives you all the strength to change the world and represent His name well.

To my 13 siblings: LaDonna, Ramona, Terry, Karen, Rudy, Rodney, Shelby, Christopher, Courtney, Leslie, Samuel, Dorcas, and Marla - you all challenge me to be my absolute best. Thank you for supporting me spiritually, physically, emotionally, mentally, and financially, without ever looking for anything in return.

To my Queen "Eagle" Scholar, Dr. Raven Jones Stanbrough: I pray that you receive 100-fold the love, care, attention to detail and literary genius you invested into this project. My newfound respect for your rare and valuable skill set has elevated to heights indescribable. You, Darryl, and my Zuri Hudson hold a special place in my heart always. Thank you from the bottom of my heart.

To my "Twin" Ashara Ylana, who knew over 30 years ago our love for each other, and friendship would bring us here? Wow. God truly hand selected you to hold my hand and encourage me through the publishing process. Your skill set is unmatched! I love you, my LST.

I'm forever grateful to each person who played a pivotal role in our marriage that kept us focused on our goals and challenged us to fight for it when things were dim. **You know exactly who you are.** It's truly a village work. Thank you!

Preface

About the book:

*M*arriage and family are by far what I'm most passionate about. Why? Marriage is like water. It affects us all in some way, shape or form daily. Healthy marriages are the solution to so many problems we face in society. Healthy marriages are the foundation to strong families, which in turn build strong communities. I found myself repeatedly saying, "Boy, I wish I knew this before I said I do..." when giving advice to people of all ages about relationships, marriage, and family. I finally decided to pen the wisdom I've attained thus far and explain the benefits of continual learning and growing. We all learn through conquering our pain and shortcomings, then make them the platform we stand on to tell our stories of triumph.

How it came to be:

I've been married for 28 years as of today and we've known each other over 32 years. I was inspired to start writing after constantly encouraging my three, young adult, creative children to, "Never be afraid to live out loud or you'll slowly die in silence." I'm also a huge Casey Neistat fan (Film Creator/YouTube) and he said this profound quote: "Without a goal, you can't score." I witness a lot of people in pain in their marriages and my goal is to give them hope. Whether you're single, engaged, married, widowed, or divorced - we're all in this together. We're tackling the same struggles and searching for the same answers. My ultimate goal is to guide you to the only One who knows what you need and cares about the struggles you face. He alone has all the answers and we ALL score.

What inspired it:

I want the readers to glean solutions from these lessons that they can apply immediately and feel confident about the results. I also want them to pen their lessons learned and share them as often as possible. We need each other's testimonies to survive! Jesus has done some wonderful things for all of us, and I believe what the word says in John 21:25, if we all wrote down what He has done, the Earth couldn't contain the books. I also want to inspire the next generation and give them a fresh perspective to draw from.

What the writing process was like:

Johann Sebastian Bach would write J.J. (Jesu Juva) at the top of his page to ask for Jesus's help in composing a score, and at the end of the page he'd write SDG (Sole Deo Gloria), meaning for the glory of God alone. I, too, share in his sentiment as the Lord walked me through each page of this book.

I approached each lesson by stating our history and how we thought at that time. Then, I provided the background, setting, and what we've learned through our school of "hard knocks." Lastly, I share how we overcame, and the maturity gained through our process. I close each lesson with a relevant prayer based on the wisdom I have today.

At times, it was daunting to relive the pain, but I wanted you to have hope, so I included every significant detail from beginning to end. However, it was also joyous to pen the victorious testimonies that I've obtained through these lessons. I pray that you ask for Jesus's help to guide you through your marriage and that God alone is glorified for its success!

Introduction

Welcome to the wonderful world of relationships, marriage, and family! I pray this book:

- Brings insight if you're anticipating marriage.
- Gives clarity and confirmation if you're searching for answers.
- Encourages you to keep going if you're losing momentum.
- Gives you hope if you're feeling hopeless and void of strength to stay in your marriage.

Most importantly, I pray it makes you laugh and not take life so seriously that you've forgotten how to have fun.

Lesson **25**

You Didn't Marry the Wrong Person

*Y*es, coming out of the gate I'm going to the very first thought I had when trouble showed up as soon as I got home from my honeymoon. It seemed as if it was greeting me at the door and all I wanted to do is open our wedding gifts.

Here I was 22 years old and thinking because we dated for four years that I learned all the major things about him. I thought whatever life threw at us, it wouldn't come as a major shock. Boy was I wrong! I remember his Mom saying on our wedding video, "…you two seem to weather the storms pretty well" and wished us her best. Our four-year dating history, while fun and exciting, was also messy and included at least three break ups. I presume her observance of us made her feel we had the tools necessary to overcome whatever life dealt us. It felt good hearing that from a key person in our village.

The answer is, a honeymoon follows a wedding, and a wedding is an event.

So why did I think I married the wrong person? A month earlier, he was perfectly suited, and all was well in the world. The answer is, a honeymoon follows a wedding, and a wedding is an event. That event is the **official** beginning, and I couldn't rely on our dating history anymore. While that foundation is important, it wasn't real or solid. Our marriage had to be built.

I love construction so I will use this analogy to explain this part of the lesson.

Picture this, you see a beautiful home complete with immaculate landscaping and gorgeous curb appeal. That's what a wedding is. A wedding is also a mere rendering that reveals what's going to be built on these grounds much like a "Future home of Target" sign. Normally, the signage will also tell you when construction will be completed and when the business will be open to the public. As a passerby, we wait in expectation for the opening day so we can patronize it.

I was clueless as if I were reading a foreign language.

For our marriage, I soon realized that the site was ready, and we had all the tools, supplies, and construction workers we needed to complete it, but we didn't know how to read the blueprints. We didn't know where to start. I had no idea how to read the blueprints titled, "Rozelle Fredrick White Jr." I was clueless as if I were reading a foreign language.

I, like most people, just started building my marriage based on other people's interpretation of what the building plans stated. I was looking at the pictures and guessing most of the time and sometimes the parts fit and other times they didn't.

As soon as conflict arose, I had a solution based on my own knowledge of the situation and so did he. So, the back and forth of whose plan we were going to follow only stopped the progress. The first thought again is, "This is a nightmare. I married the wrong person, and something is wrong with him/her!"

The hardest part is determining who's going to be the general contractor on this (marriage) construction project and that's where the fighting and arguments began.

At 18 years old when I met Rozelle, I had a picture of what I thought marriage was supposed to look like and that picture came directly from my view of my parents. They'd been married 24 years at that time, and I viewed their marriage as solid and strong. My parents met when they were teens and married a few years later. They had 14 children (seven sons and seven daughters) and I'm the fifth eldest.

My Dad was strong and very firm. He was dedicated to my Mom and us, and I believe part of that dedication stemmed from a lack of dedication that he witnessed from his Dad's marriage to his mother. His father died when he was eleven years old, and later his Mom met and married a wonderful man who was an awesome stepfather for my Dad. He learned a lot from seeing a loving, stable relationship from his Mom's second marriage.

My Mom had a similar story to his, one that I believe brought them together. Her father wasn't the best husband to my grandmother and father to their children. After he died, her Mom remarried an awesome man that restored her faith in true love and commitment.

Growing up in my household was an experience. It was the epitome of love, fun, and laughter mixed with our fair share of pain, sadness, and sibling rivalry. Our parents instilled in us that "all we have on this Earth are our brothers and sisters." They were dedicated Christians and faith was the true foundation of our home.

Naturally, I felt I was better qualified to be the general contractor on our building site called the "Future Home of the White House." Boy was I dead wrong! I couldn't read the blueprints and I abandoned them and used what I saw work from my childhood home. In some areas I was successful, in others not so much.

Our first arguments were about money. Who was best suited to manage the finances? Well, my husband, who was pursuing his bachelor's in business administration felt he was professionally qualified. After a few months of watching how he managed finances and paid bills, I knew this wasn't going to work. All I could see was my Dad all over again. My Dad wasn't a good money manager. My Mom was more organized and structured, and that was a huge point of contention and a source of many arguments in our home when we were younger.

I was irate when Rozelle wouldn't let me manage the finances and the fights were epic. In our early years, we eventually settled on the "roommate" plan which was splitting everything down the middle. This didn't solve the issue, but it kept us from arguing so much. I wasn't at peace at all because I realized that avoidance was our coping mechanism for a lot of our issues while sweeping things under the rug. I soon noticed that this became our approach for a lot of our issues. Separation. Because we agreed on being separate, it worked, no matter how counterproductive it was.

I also saw my parents argue all the time when I was younger and as I got older, they argued a lot less. They worked things out and laughed a lot, so I didn't see arguing as destructive. Rozelle didn't grow up this way and arguing was damaging from his perspective. He would do one of two things; verbally abuse to close down the conversation or go totally silent.

Within a few months, I noticed we mastered the art of not communicating at all.

Within a few months, I noticed we mastered the art of not communicating at all. We talked all the time, but we avoided sensitive conversations. Communication is:

- When both parties hear the other and walk away with a clear understanding of what each other is conveying.
- When both people can repeat back to each other what their expectations and goals are.

We didn't know how to communicate so we settled for talking. Talking is telling the other person what you want them to know without an emotional connection or regard for their input. Talking is easy and what we do with our coworkers and neighbors. Talking is minimalist and gets directly to the point. In those early years, we mastered the art of talking. Talking kept the tension away and made for a much better environment in our home.

So here we are, newlyweds and we opted for separation, avoidance and talking. These building tools are based on feelings, emotions, and pride. They make for a slow, counter-productive building project with major confusion and division. We needed to unite, communicate, and face the uncomfortable pain from our childhoods before we could ever build a lasting marriage on a firm foundation. We needed to allow the **only** General Contractor who knew, wrote, and could interpret our plans, to take over our building site. Jeremiah 29:11 says His plans for us are <u>all</u> good.

It's amazing what we do when we're convinced that we're right, and our spouse is wrong.

Fortunately, one thing that was constant amid our chaos was our friendship. We really liked to hang out with each other and have fun. Early on, we adopted choosing friendship over being spouses. It was the answer to peace and "if I married the wrong person." It's amazing what we do when we're convinced that we're right, and our spouse is wrong. As friends, we were both waiting for the other to figure out that "I am right", and in the meantime all the dysfunction continues.

So, here's the truth; clearly, I didn't marry the wrong person, I just didn't know what I was doing, and I was full of pride.

There's only One master builder and He's the creator of marriage. We waste time when we don't consult Him in all we do and rely on our own knowledge. We waste even more time using all the schools of thought from the world and other people. God is specific and incredibly detailed. He had a plan for us, and He wanted to be consulted for the entire process. Most importantly, He loved us enough to continue to draw us with lovingkindness despite our pride and ignorance.

I didn't know that I was being broken and crushed so that I could be formed into one with Rozelle.

You're the product of all your combined childhood experiences. I didn't know that I was being broken and crushed so that I could be formed into **one** with Rozelle. Everything I thought I knew had to be tested, tried, and placed in the fiery kiln of marriage. No one on this Earth can fully comprehend what the process will be to **become** one in marriage but the Lord. Those early uncomfortable days drove us to Him and His word.

We both loved God and believed His word but not at the level of experience needed to be married. There were key things that should've been completed as single people that we didn't do. (I examine these things in Lesson 24.) Jesus wasn't Lord of our lives as single people and it was exposed immediately in our marriage.

Jesus said in Luke 6:46-49 when He references building a house, that you call me Lord, Lord but don't do the things I say. When you have two people determined to do things their own way and show the other that they're wrong, it's just a matter of time that so much dissension and division develops that it seems impossible to work through. We did things our own way without consulting the Lord prior to marriage and that didn't automatically stop once we were married.

I didn't know then that the very first step to building a marriage was demolishing the existing structures. Those structures were me and Rozelle. We individually had to be torn down in our ways of thinking and crushed under the weight of our earthly knowledge. Then, we were to be ground down to a fine powder that the Lord could use on His potter's wheel. When this process is happening in the Spirit, in the natural it appears as fighting, arguing, crying, pointing fingers, and placing blame.

It's a pain that's inexplicable. A pain so heavy you can literally touch it. The weight of it at times seems insurmountable and it strips you of all hope. The natural inclination is to run away and abandon your "job site" as many do, which explains the divorce rate. When you're facing that pain, day in and day out, even the strongest of the strong can collapse under its weight. There is only one solution: surrendering to it.

Let me explain why this breaking, crushing and surrendering is so imperative; two people are becoming one.

In the King James Version of Matthew 19:5, it says,...and the two shall become one flesh. Let's look closely at the definitions of the words SHALL and BECOME. They're both verbs.

- **Shall:**
  - (in the first person) expressing the future tense
  - means expressing an instruction or command

- **Become:**
  - begin to be
  - (of a person) qualify or be accepted as
  - acquire the status of

Jesus was specifically talking to married individuals. In keeping with the definitions above He was saying, *"In the future you will begin to be one person through a process called marriage, which will qualify you to acquire the status of being joined together by God."*

Marriage is a process designed to expose and qualify you. You consented to be exposed when you said, "I do." However, you can't qualify if you don't first pass the test of surrendering to the One who created marriage.

You recall that this passage was about Jesus addressing a Pharisee who asked Him about divorce. Jesus wanted married people to know that their commitment to each other was going to be tested and it was going to be a process to become one. That process begins with being exposed. He knew the natural tendency of human beings when they face pain and conflict, is to entertain reasons why they should "put each other away" so He addressed the matter plainly. In verse 8, He says the root, or the origin of divorce is:

1. Hardness of heart
2. Lack of commitment to the process

Those individuals who lack commitment to surrendering **to God** in their marriage, will face divorce, but they don't have to.

> **This surgical process is in reverse when you get married. It's a spiritual surgery to take two different people and join them together as one person.**

In this passage of scripture, Jesus also talks about two people becoming one flesh. It was a surgical procedure to remove Eve from Adam in Genesis as they were already one person. They were perfectly joined together functioning as one flesh until God removed Eve from him.

Now let's shift the comparison to marriage to undergoing surgery.

This surgical process is in reverse when you get married. It's a spiritual surgery to take two different people and join them together as one person. God is the master surgeon and Jesus's blood is the transfusion product. Blood is the source of life and when surgeries happen in the natural, the surgeon ensures there's enough blood product on hand for the patient to replace what is lost during the procedure. Additionally, it's impossible to be awake during a surgical procedure, you must be put to sleep just as Adam was. In marriage, you must trust the master surgeon, which is God Himself to perform this spiritual process. You must be put to sleep (totally surrendered) before He can do His best work in you.

In the natural, surgery can't take place unless the consent is read and signed. You said "Yes" or "I do" at the altar and gave your consent when signing your marriage license. Now, you must go under anesthesia (be put to sleep) so the surgeon can operate.

- Are you in pain in your marriage?
- Are you still awake?
- Remember, you gave the Lord consent for this surgery at the altar when you said, "I do".
- You can't endure this process unless you're sleep (totally surrendered.)

In this passage of scripture Jesus also talks about divorce being connected to a hard heart. Let's look at this process from a physical heart for greater emphasis.

Corresponding to Strong's Greek 464, hard-heartedness is:

- Feminine of a compound of skleros and kardia
- Skleros means hard
- Kardia means heart
- (Etymology) Skleros is pertaining to the tissue changes or other factors involved in the progress of sclerosis of the heart
- Destitute of perception

According to Mosby's Medical Dictionary, 9th edition, hardheartedness is, tissue changes that cause the heart walls and/or arteries to thicken and block blood flow.

In connection to the definitions above, hardheartedness in the spirit is becoming destitute of perception, which is a choice to NOT allow the Lord to correct what's wrong, thus the heart can't receive what it needs to survive. Destitute of perception means you make a choice not to see, hear or become aware through your senses.

Therefore, when a man or woman chooses to harden their heart toward their spouse, they're cutting off their life source and refusing to follow through with the process of becoming one through surgery/marriage.

Imagine as you were saying your vows you were being sown together in a spiritual surgery. When you surrender to the Lord in your marriage, you're giving Him permission to operate and remove, repair, or replace what's causing your hardness of heart.

Can you imagine waking up after being connected to your spouse in a surgery? It's painful after the medication (honeymoon phase) wears off.

Can you imagine waking up after being connected to your spouse in a surgery? It's painful after the medication (honeymoon phase) wears off. Just like in the natural, you must undergo a lot of physical therapy and follow the instructions that the surgeon gives you.

When we get married, we think we're supposed to instantly live a life together without pain and discomfort. That's impossible. You just underwent a major surgery! However, if you follow the instructions you minimize the pain and heal timely and properly. We must surrender and follow the instructions that God gives us, and we **shall** become one over time.

Another example in the natural, when we're in pain, our bodies are telling us that something isn't functioning as designed. That pain drives us to seek medical attention because it's not normal. When married couples are becoming one, and all the junk in our minds is being processed and renewed, it's painful as well. This pain should drive us to seek the attention of the only One who has the answers.

Your marriage is designed to expose and rid of all those things that'll prohibit the two of you from becoming one.

This is the real work of marriage. In the Spirit, God removes all the things that aren't healthy and replaces all the vital things you need to live whole and free. You don't even know what you've stored in your mind and why you think and act the way you do, but God does. Your marriage is designed to expose and rid of all those things that'll prohibit the two of you from becoming one.

The bible shows us that the heart and mind are connected (Psalm 64:6). They work in tandem. Your heart has so many hidden chambers that only God can know and accurately diagnose it. This work can only be done through the Spirit. The Holy Spirit helps our weaknesses, but we must ask Him for help.

The Word cautions us not to divide ourselves or let any person or thing divide us as married couples. In the *Berean Study Bible* Mark 10:9 says … what God has joined, let no man separate. That man Jesus speaks about is **you**. Don't you separate yourself from your spouse due to a hard heart.

Rozelle and I say all the time that we enjoyed our wedding on March 19, 1993, but it took years for us to qualify, accept, and acquire the status of married. It took years for us and others to say, "marriage becomes us."

The Lord, in His infinite wisdom, had a good plan for the two of us that we couldn't see at the time. It wasn't until:

- We surrendered to His will and dismissed all our pride that we started to see real progress.
- We decided to do what He said specifically for our marriage that we had peace in our home.
- I stopped looking at Rozelle as the issue and asked the Lord to show me myself that I saw tremendous progress.
- I prayed "Lord, heal me everywhere I hurt" that me and my entire family began to experience healing and life God's way.

I went to sleep (totally surrendered) and allowed the Master Surgeon to do His best work in me.

Clearly, I didn't marry the wrong person, marriage was doing what it was designed to do; expose, qualify and form us into one over time. I went to sleep (totally surrendered) and allowed the Master Surgeon to do His best work in me.

If you're reading this lesson and you're in pain and feeling hopeless, you don't need your spouse to surrender with you, you can do it by YOURSELF. You can agree with the Lord that you need healing and start working on yourself immediately. You can swallow your pride and everything you think you know and let the Lord teach you the specific plan He has for you.

You have plenty of work to do that your spouse can't do for you, so do your work, and stop keeping track of what they're not doing. You're wasting time by arguing, pointing fingers, and keeping track and you're being deceived into believing you <u>don't</u> have a role in your problems. That's hard heartedness in its simplest form.

Surrender today and give the Master Surgeon consent to work on you. You'll be amazed as you watch the plan of God unfold for your marriage. It's going to be the best decision you'll ever make!

Hurry, generations are waiting on you!

Let's pray:

Lord, from this moment forward, I won't speak death to my marriage and say I married the wrong person. I know you have a plan for me. I know you have a plan for us. Holy Spirit help me destroy all the things and schools of thought that'll be destructive to my marriage. Help me search my heart and heal me everywhere I hurt. You're the Only source of wisdom and you're here to teach me all things. Lord, you created marriage and you have the master plan for MY marriage. I realize I'm building a foundation and it's the most important part of the building process. I want my foundation to be firm and stable so that you can build a future generation upon it for **your** glory alone. Thank you, Lord, for connecting me with married people who are winning and transparent about how you've helped them grow together. I commit to talking to you Lord about my marriage more than **anyone** else. I'll listen when you instruct me and do what you tell me to do. I won't make the choice to harden my heart. Today and every day I'll surrender to this process of becoming one with my spouse. I'm strong and well-equipped to fulfill my commitment with your help. In Jesus's name, Amen.

Lesson 24

Alone Work Is Not an Option

*T*he Bible refers to a yoke in several books of the Old Testament. A yoke is a wooden crosspiece that's fastened over the necks of two animals and attached to the plow or cart that they're to pull. To maximize the efficiency of this process, the animals were paired in size, strength, and height.

I got married in 1993, and in my church community it wasn't uncommon to marry young. The criteria for marriage were simple; make sure you're equally yoked and love each other. Equally yoked at that time for me meant, both parties served our Lord and Savior Jesus Christ and believed in the person and power of the Holy Spirit. Everything else was personal preference.

Rozelle was all the above and an awfully hard worker. Work ethic was crucial for me because I witnessed my Dad work hard for years at Ford Motor Company to provide for us, and he even went to work ill on many occasions. Rozelle was also educated and enjoyed learning. When I met him, he was working three jobs and maintaining a 4.0 GPA in college. We had a lot in common and had a lot of fun together. When you consider my maturity level at the time, I agreed Rozelle and I were equal in size, strength, height, and capable of "pulling" the load of marriage.

I didn't know how pivotal my purpose was at this time, nor do I think it was ever explained to me the way I heard Myles Munroe state in his sermon, "Keys to Fulfilling your Vision." He exclaimed, "You were created to solve a problem on this Earth and that is your purpose. God walked through and finished your life story then He started production the day you were born."

I was 44 years old when I heard this revelation for the first time. It was a game changer. I prayed about it and that's when the Lord showed me that my purpose was to begin as Stacey Lyn Prater; a grown, single woman with zero responsibilities. I didn't need anyone else's help to discover and begin this work except the Holy Spirit. This was a crucial step I didn't realize.

I was led to search the scriptures about the parable of the talents (Matthew 25:14-30) and that's when I learned that everything I needed for my single-person work is here and waiting on me. Provision means "for the vision." Everything for my vision is already here, and I was created afterwards. Just like in creation, God created the heavens, Earth, seas, animals, day, and evening BEFORE He created Man.

Man was given a place to live, food to eat, time to track day and evenings and most importantly, what he was created to do with his life.

God gave him his precise purpose and work and provided everything needed to successfully accomplish it.

This new revelation was fascinating to me. I was curious to know what I was to accomplish as a single person that I didn't finish before I got married, therefore I was looking to fill this void elsewhere.

Here's a little backstory to my life prior to marriage:

> When my mother died suddenly in 1991, my whole world was flipped upside down, I was in shock, and beyond devastated. In my despair, I questioned God repeatedly. I was 21 years old in college on an academic/work scholarship. I immediately began to make reckless choices and sabotaged my education. Those reckless choices and unbridled grief resulted in me losing my scholarship and being kicked out of school in Tennessee, then I headed back home to Michigan. I started working full-time and took college classes part time. It was one of the darkest times of my life. I was angry at God and trying to find purpose in moving forward with life. Everything I'd been taught was being tested. I continued going to church and working during my stages of shock and grief, but nothing seemed to comfort this gargantuan hole in my heart.

At this time, Rozelle and I had been dating on and off for about two years and I was done with that drama, so I called off our engagement for the second time. One day, I was working for my sister at her salon and she and a few of her clients were discussing a book they were reading by Benny Hinn titled, *Good Morning, Holy Spirit* (1990).

I was skeptical but I bought it and started reading it. It was an outstanding read. It helped me to vocalize and heal from the unbearable pain I was feeling by talking audibly to the Holy Spirit daily. "It" became a "He." A person. Someone I considered a friend.

I started growing more and the pain of my Mom's absence was, for the first time, bearable.

Rozelle was still around. We hung out from time to time, and we went to the same church, so we saw each other often. Perhaps, he was a security blanket because he knew my Mom and my family, and I didn't have to preface any conversations about my grief with a back story when talking to him about her.

In July of 1992, I finished reading the book and one morning I woke up and drove to Rozelle's apartment. I told him that I was done playing with my relationship with God and that I was going to be steadfast on my goal to grow in God. He too, had a similar conversation with God a few days earlier. We talked about the book at length, so he purchased it and read it too. A few months later, we decided that we'd get married the next year in March. It would be four years to the day that we met, March 19th.

Now, this is where the wisdom I have now comes into play. The Holy Spirit was clearly speaking to us and giving us direction for our individual lives. We were investing in our personal relationships with the Lord, and we were beginning to see fruit. We should've kept moving forward in that direction because what we were supposed to do as single, individual people would've been revealed. Instead, two unfulfilled single people decided to get married with incomplete single assignments.

We should've kept moving forward in that direction because what we were supposed to do as single, individual people would've been revealed.

Genesis 2:18 shows that God created Eve after Adam asked for help. Help with what exactly? Help with his harvest from working. I love how Myles Munroe explains this in his book titled, *Understanding the Purpose and Power of Men* (2001). In the garden of Eden, the Lord didn't allow for rain to fall or his harvest to bloom because there was no one to manage it. Adam needed help to manage his work and Eve was perfectly equipped and suited to do so. They were all in one, so she witnessed everything Adam had already accomplished prior to be separated from him.

Rozelle and I hadn't learned to manage our own lives and finish our single work first. Our single work was to produce a harvest that would require help in the proper season.

Genesis 2:20-21 mentions Adam needing suitable help. Helpmeet is a compound of two words: help and meet. Help in this verse implies assistance with something, not being rescued. If I need help, it's because I've already been productive and now require assistance from someone of equal size, strength, and height moving forward. Meet is a verb meaning collide or connect. In the most literal sense, if I'm meeting someone, it indicates that I must move and be productive to get to the meeting place. Our harvests from our single work should've been "equal in size, strength, and height" positioning us to pull the weight of marriage.

We missed this crucial step and like many, didn't understand what the Word of God was stating in Genesis.

When God said, be fruitful, and multiply. There is a comma behind fruitful.

Producing fruit is the first step. We didn't have much fruit and we didn't know what our individual purposes were at that time. Our individual purposes were to produce fruit and a harvest over time, that would eventually require a "help meeting."

In Genesis 2, it also said that Adam was **alone** not lonely. There's a difference between the two words. Alone is a great thing. Alone is derived from the Middle English definition of "all in one." We often confuse alone with lonely, as lonely has a negative connotation. That's not the reference that God was making in Genesis 1:27. When God created them and blessed them, it shows that He was speaking about two people who were **all in one**. They were together and whole. God said it is not good for man to be (alone) all in one, I will make a help meet (suitable) for him. Adam had a relationship with the Father first, he spent time with Him and knew what he was created to do.

Our society gives the opposite definition of single and stresses that we should be searching for a mate during this time. We don't teach that we're to be accountable for our time and we should have tangible fruit from our single work, with a visible yearly harvest.

During this time, we should be unwavering in seeking the Lord for our individual, specific work He created us to be the solutions for. This is the foundation that marriage is to be built upon. In addition to that, we're to work through our childhood issues and get rid of the pain we carry deep in our hearts. This establishes discipline and trust in God.

I strongly believe this is one of the many reasons divorce happens. There are a lot of single men and single women who haven't been fruitful (naturally and spiritually) to a point where their individual harvest requires help (multiplying.)

Then we replace our single work with marriage.

We soon discover that marriage isn't for the undisciplined and unfulfilled single person. Far too often, we associate being fruitful with pursuing careers and financial success and this isn't the totality of what God intended. If it were, then the void we carry into our marriages wouldn't exist. Careers and finances are just one small piece of the puzzle. You must show fruit and continual harvests in your health, your family relationships, your spiritual walk as well as your career/finances. I elaborate more on these four areas in Lesson 14. Being fruitful requires discipline.

I wasn't disciplined and neither was Rozelle when we got married, and when you calculate zero fruit on top of a lack of discipline, you're asking for a lot of unnecessary pain, fights, and agony. Learning to discipline yourself in the four areas above is so much harder once you're married. It's possible, but you're going to have to balance everything you're currently responsible for while mastering this mandatory foundational key.

Discovering and completing our single work:

- Would begin the process of fulfilling our purposes for being here on Earth.
- Would include being whole mentally and emotionally as well as financially.
- Was to produce a harvest that would require help, then we were to get married.
- Would be the foundation we needed to build our lives on as a married couple.
- Is cumulative and would be a catalyst for the work we were to do as a married couple.

Our single-all-in-one (alone) work **doesn't** go away just because we didn't know the Word of God and that it was mandatory. We still carried it around inside of us, and the void from not doing it grows greater with time. The provision is already here, and it's waiting for us to access it.

I wonder how many people like me at the time, are walking around looking for a person, place, thing, job, or geographical location to fulfill a void, that only your specifically designed purpose can.

I strongly believe most couples can't articulate the void they feel from a lack of discipline and leaving this work incomplete.

These voids mask themselves in arguments, disagreements, resentment, and lack of contentment.

It's nearly impossible to be on one accord when the enemy uses this, and many other strategies to keep couples divided. The good news is, once you identify this problem, it's easy to overcome it with God's help.

There's a problem on this Earth that God created **you** to solve and equipped you with everything you need to solve it. This problem will remain until you consult the **only** person who has your plan. His name is Jesus.

If you're already married, it's never too late to find out what you didn't complete as a single-all-in-one-person. I know you'll discover that it'll fulfill you and bring joy to you first, then your marriage and family. I'm sure you, like me, will find that the happiness and contentment you were searching for from your spouse or other outside things, will come from discovering and remaining dedicated to this work. Principally, the kingdom will be advanced from your obedience and this is the supreme goal.

The time is now so don't delay, put maximum effort into finding out what you were purposed to do and then do it. The Bible warns us about being hearers only and not doing what we know to do (James 1:22).

To my single men and women, you're blessed to find this key information out now <u>before</u> getting married. Now that you know better, get started today! Surround yourself with people who'll hold you accountable to your work and connect with them often.

Fasting brings you true knowledge of your God-given purpose and sound healing.

Whether single or married, I highly recommend going on a fast and consecrating yourself. The *Berean Study Bible* of Isaiah 58:8 says, then your light will break forth like the dawn, and your healing will come quickly. Light is also known as knowledge. Healing is also known as becoming sound, well founded, well-grounded and proper. Fasting brings you true knowledge of your God-given purpose and sound healing.

The *Pulpit Commentary* of this verse states, "When thou hast taken this advice (proper fasting) to heart, and adopted it, and made it the rule of thy conduct. Upon such a change in thee, all good things shall follow. Thou shalt have no more to complain of unanswered prayers or covenant promises left in abeyance (suspension).

I agree with this statement wholeheartedly. You're going to change for the better, good things will follow your change and no more voids from unanswered prayers! Fasting is where you'll obtain precise instructions and directions, so be sure to write them down for reference and answerability to remain on track. Your best life awaits you and generations need your solution to the problems they'll face!

Let's pray:

Father, I thank you for the purpose you have given me. Thank you for giving me a helper in the person of the Holy Spirit that I can rely on to accomplish this work. I understand, just like the Master in the parable of the talents, you're coming back expecting a harvest from what you've given me. I'm well able, funded, and supported so I won't give you any excuses. Thank you for sending the resources I need and like-minded believers to encourage me as I move forward with my purpose work. I commit to spending time with you so I can clearly hear your voice. After I receive my next steps, I won't attempt any part of your plans using my own intellect. I'm excited and looking forward to hearing you say "Well done" for my single-all-in-one-work I accomplished with the help of the Holy Spirit only. In Jesus's name, Amen.

Lesson 23

Death, Burial, and Resurrection

The *New Living Translation* of John 12:24 says, I tell you the truth, unless a kernel of wheat is planted in the soil and dies, it remains alone. But its death will produce many new kernels—a plentiful harvest of new lives.

Wow. That's a lot packed into that scripture.

One of the thoughts processes I had to learn, and be reprogrammed in, was sex within marriage.

Jesus was referring to His death in that scripture however, seeds can be human thought processes as well. It's how you understand and process information. So, what I learned in my marriage is I needed to be willing to die to my thought processes, and plant myself underground (in the Word of God) where the nutrients for new, healthy root systems are established. One of the thoughts processes I had to learn, and be reprogrammed in, was sex within marriage.

I love simplicity when I study so I began researching seeds. I also love documentaries and my research led me to a video on YouTube from the Moody Science Institute. Their videos date back to the 80's and I enjoy the one titled, *Journey of Life* (1985). One of the segments illustrate how different seeds are formed and the process they undergo to find ground to root themselves. It demonstrated how some seeds replenish themselves and how they travel with the help of the wind and humankind. It's a fascinating process! A major message from this documentary that resonated with me was, no seed can reach its full potential above ground. It must be buried.

Equipped with this knowledge, I was faced with a tough decision. Would I be willing to submit to the process of dying to all I knew and believed, so I could be formed and rooted into one with Rozelle? This is a lengthy process and it's more difficult if you resist it. As a 22-year-old newlywed, I had no clue that this was the goal. I had to release everything that didn't align with the Word of God concerning sex within my marriage. Some of the things I assimilated from my family and community, no matter how well it worked for them, I still had to discard it. It felt like a death too.

All you've obtained and consider noteworthy is a non-factor when building the marriage God planned for you.

What about all the things, and schools of thought we adopt from society that we bring to our marriage? Well, all those had to die as well. All you've obtained and consider noteworthy is a non-factor when building the marriage God planned for you. Like Paul said, I count my knowledge as garbage in my quest to know Christ (Philippians 3:8.) We had our own unique, God-created soil that had all the nutrients **we** needed to germinate, root, and eventually break ground.

Far too often couples fight for so long in this area because they feel the problem is with their spouse and not them. The fighting over who should change can go on for years and years and that's when division creeps in. Division means there are two visions, two opinions or two schools of thoughts. However, when you divide them by the **only** truth, which is the Word of God, you're left with one. One person that the two of you died to become.

Here's a specific example of death, burial, and resurrection concerning sex for us:

> We both came from two different backgrounds and how we were introduced to sex was totally different. I was raised in the church and taught that sex was created by God and designed for married couples. Rozelle wasn't brought up in the church and was introduced to sex as a young boy. Like most boys, their first introduction is pornography and/or masturbation.

Rozelle accepted Jesus as his Lord and Savior as a child but didn't become Spirit filled until he was 21 years old. I was 18 when I met him and inexperienced with sex. After dating for a year, we started a sexual relationship, and our goal was to be married after I finished college. While I knew the teachings about sex and what the Word of God said about it, I didn't **fully** understand why God strictly created it for marriage. I didn't do any further research either. In my mind, we loved each other and were committed to be together and that was enough for me.

It wasn't until I left to attend college out of state that the complications began. I had a lot of friends and hung out with them and when they weren't with me; they were hanging with their significant others. Rozelle and I tried to maintain a long-distance relationship, but it was harder than I thought it'd be.

Through a series of unfortunate events that I detail in Lessons 2 and 6, we decided to break up. The break-up-get-back-together cycle had begun in our relationship and it was extremely hurtful to the other people we involved. We broke up one time and determined that we shouldn't remain friends either because it was so complicated. I was devastated. I couldn't understand why I was so upset. I tried to busy myself with work and school, but it didn't help.

> ## While sex has a few distinct purposes, the one that reappeared to me was, it's a covenant relationship.

I came home over the summer and decided I'd stay to myself instead of getting into a new relationship. It was then that I re-read a book by Edwin Louis Cole titled *Communication, Sex and Money* (1987). I had the privilege of hearing this accomplished author speak at our church a few years earlier and he was astounding. I dug into the chapters on sex and discovered why the Lord structured it the way He did. While sex has a few distinct purposes, the one that reappeared to me was, it's a covenant relationship. Louis Cole explains how sex was designed to build and bond two people together. This bond is beyond the physical realm and has a deeply spiritual origin. I'd connected myself with Rozelle and didn't understand the process of breaking up involved much more than just saying "We're done."

> ## This is an emotional and psychological connection most men and women feel but can't adequately explain.

I began to search the scriptures to learn what God intended through sex and decide if I was going to follow His way or my own way. It was a difficult decision. The more I learned, the more I was accountable to what I learned. I started comparing how the world views sex versus how it was created, and I began to understand why people sought to hurt those who betrayed them. This is an emotional and psychological connection most men and women feel but can't adequately explain. When that connection is broken the human heart/mind must go through a complete disconnection process. Unfortunately, most people in turn, act out in hurt, anger, and sometimes rage.

We eventually married a few years later and the roots of our sexual relationships had to be uprooted. This is something I had no idea was necessary. What we thought we knew had to be dismissed (die) and we needed to learn about sex the way God intended it specifically for **our** marriage. When you solely rely on books, research and talking with your friends about your relationship, it only complicates things. You're essentially applying second-hand knowledge to a one-of-a-kind relationship.

I like to use the analogy that sex within a marriage is as specialized and one-of-a-kind as your teeth. Your teeth and how they were designed to fit **your** jaw bones, mouth and facial structure were formed by your Creator alone. No one else on this Earth has your teeth. They also require care specialized to you. Sex in your marriage is just that meticulous. While general sexual knowledge is common, there are areas we're responsible for discovering on our own from the One who created us and sex. We couldn't rely on what worked before our marriage or what worked for other people.

It was intricate and draining to dig into what Rozelle and I replaced sex with that it wasn't intended for.

It was intricate and draining to dig into what Rozelle and I replaced sex with that it wasn't intended for. It was also a reality check to have to cut those soul ties with former partners even though there was no physical communication or connections with them anymore. These further cements the fact that sex is spiritual, emotional, and psychological.

In a 2010 YouTube sermon, Myles Munroe preached, "Why Men Need Dreams & Visions," regarding relationships. He shared that he waited to

45

have sex with his wife for several reasons. One of the main ones was, he witnessed a lot of his friends who had sexual partners prior to marriage, have so many self-disciplinary issues to contend with post marriage.

> ## Marriage is not an all-inclusive solution for a lack of self-discipline in this area.

Research shows that most Christian people are introduced to sex between the ages of 11-14 years and never taught the specific biblical reasons why God created it. Consequently, this becomes our strongest appetite outside of food, and it controls us instead of us having discipline over it. As time goes on, coupled with secular views, we foster relationships with people based solely on sex first. Exercising discipline in this area is inexistent for most people, married or otherwise. The self-control assignment in this area didn't just go away because we got married. Marriage is not an all-inclusive solution for a lack of self-discipline in this area. Rozelle and I individually needed to learn self-discipline (temperance) and it was a complicated process.

In addition, Munroe stated that in learning self-control, "you still have to deal with your memory." I agree with him. I had to be taught self-control and surrender my thought life to the Lord concurrently. That required me to first deal with many underlying factors such as: lust, manipulation, and pride. My old, twisted, and perverted thought patterns and what I considered to be truth had to die.

So as newlyweds, two major components were missing and/or flawed. Communication and self-control. At that time, we were poor communicators at best. Great talkers but poor communicators, so this process took years because all growth in a marriage requires communication first. We didn't know the connection between communication and sex. Communication precedes sex and one can't exist without the other. God's approach to sex and healthy communication had to grow and be cultivated. Across time and seasons, it produced good healthy fruit that was perfect for us. Like all healthy, fruit-bearing trees, they need to be pruned so they can **continue** producing good fruit season after season.

The Lord in his wisdom and sovereignty created opportunities for us to grow and conquer in these areas. I read a lot of books and received a lot of wise counsel, but the best counsel I received was, "Stacey, you must obtain the answers that were specifically created for you and Rozelle."

That advice was profound, and I likened it to a key. Many keys look alike and if you aligned them next to each other, you can't see any noticeable differences, but the locksmith can. He knows every notch, groove, and divot that matches the lock it was **designed** to open. We had a hand-crafted key, cut by the Lord Himself for our marriage, and I was determined to receive it and access what was ours.

> **His designed and purpose for sex within our marriage succeeded and I value it just like a key to a priceless vault.**

None of the above was attainable without fasting and prayer.

For a season, it seemed like all I did was back-to-back fasts. God talked to me about me and built me up in those seasons. He gave me directions and answers that's had an impact on my life for YEARS. In addition to fasting and prayer, I also studied Jewish culture and their entire process of engagement through marriage because the Bible compares this process to Christ and the church. Through my studies, I learned so much about myself and Rozelle. As the Lord promised, His way and purpose will always be victorious (Job 42:2) and it was within us. His designed and purpose for sex within our marriage succeeded and I value it just like a key to a priceless vault. No one else in the world has our key nor will they ever. It's one of a kind.

Our communication flourished and continues to year after year. We understand that this major element also has a lifelong-maintenance-plan which keeps us humble and in touch with the Father. Our intimacy and sex life were totally re-built on Godly principles. It too, requires pruning and prayer to remain healthy. We can never get comfortable and stop working toward optimal health in this area because that's when challenges arise. We embraced the fact that no one else on Earth has the key to our success but the Lord, and we always win when we consult His purpose for our one-of-a-kind marriage.

I pray you've grasped that burial is a good thing! Seeds that are buried are temporarily unseen, but so much transformation is happening below ground. This crucial step of the growth process cannot be rushed. Once a seed is buried, patience and speaking life is essential to guarantee the fruit of what you've planted. Don't become impatient and dig the seed up. That causes damage and most seeds don't recover from this trauma.

Death comes before life. Jesus modeled this for us. Be willing to die to all you know, and all you **think** you know, so that the Creator of your marriage can re-educate and re-train you for your one-of-a-kind union.

I always tell people I counsel, that the time they invest in sowing will have years of returns that'll last for generations. This is precisely why you must be patient and go through the process.

Let's pray:

Lord, I thank you for highlighting my need for your resurrection power in my marriage. By faith, my marriage is healed and whole and I'll specifically do what you tell me to do to ensure its success. I thank you that you continue to show me what needs to die, be buried, and patiently await **you** to resurrect in my marriage. Lord, communication with you is essential because you have the master plan. I receive your plan and I won't allow the enemy to cut our communication ties. I'll connect with those who love marriage the way you intended, and they'll be my accountability and support in this season of growth. I won't be consumed in doubt and anger. I thank you for peace and love. I'll fast and pray. I'll seek you wholeheartedly which means I'll put maximum effort into this process. Holy Spirit give me strength when I get weary. I want the best for me and my spouse, and I recognize the Creator of marriage has a one-of-a-kind plan just for us. Lord, I'm willing and ready to die because your resurrection power extends not only for me, but for generations to come. In Jesus's name, Amen.

Lesson 22

"Something Clicked!"

When you and your spouse are in harmony it feels like a perfect sunny day. However, when things are awry, it's akin to a dark, sub-below winter day and those days seem so much longer than 24 hours.

In our early years, managing our marriage from so many of ideas, schools of thought, and advice from varied outside sources caused us major frustration. Some worked and some didn't. The frustration from the things that didn't work would cause me so much unrest.

That frustration, I now know is what was designed to steer us back to the Lord for **His** perfect plan.

From time to time, we'd say to each other, "Something clicked Babe," and that was our way of knowing we accomplished something together. Perhaps we found a solution to a problem or went to another level in our marriage. Most times these "clicks" weren't physically visible. We knew by how we felt that we were headed in the right direction. It was encouraging and gave us more fuel to keep going.

Most challenges are never welcomed but they're really opportunities for growth in disguise.

Every marriage and every married person must continually grow and learn. Learning requires challenges. Most challenges are never welcomed but they're really opportunities for growth in disguise. These challenges bring answers to the things we're praying for and believing God to heal. Healing rarely comes packaged the way we want it but if we trust Him, the outcome is perfect.

In a season of preparing for this lesson, the Lord told me "I worshiped Rozelle." I immediately said, "No way Lord, that's impossible, ugh not him!" He calmly showed me a pattern of behavior that I developed over the years that was ingrained in my mind as normal. It, in fact, was worship. I touched on this in Lesson 17, but I'll elaborate further here.

Let's define worship. Worship is:

- What or who we deem more worthy (full of worth) than God.
- What or who we place value on.
- What or who we constantly think about and/or preoccupies our thoughts.
- What or who we bend or adjust our lives around.
- What or who causes our moods, attitudes, and dispositions to change negatively or positively.

After gaining an understanding of worship from this viewpoint, I definitely needed to make some changes. I was charged with researching and studying His first commandment in Exodus 20, you shall have no other gods before me. God (our Father) means all sustaining One and Creator. In this commandment, He was instructing us to never worship things that He created or sustains. Naturally, our minds go directly to some statue made of stone, an object or thing. We rarely associate **people** with worship, but we do worship people based on the definition above.

I never thought I placed him above God, but I did.

In my case and in accordance with the definition:

- I deemed Rozelle and my marriage valuable and full of worth.
- I thought about him constantly (not always in a good way) and adjusted my life around him.
- Sadly, he did cause my mood, attitude, and disposition to greatly change negatively or positively.

I never thought I placed him above God, but I did. I was guilty of worshipping something He created rather than my Creator.

Now what's alarming, I thought I was **supposed** to do these things and that they were noteworthy. I thought this was a part of the outward display of love and respect for my husband as the Word says. Once the Lord explained the true definition of worship to me, I was floored. I asked the Lord again, "Okay, exactly how has my pattern of thinking manifested itself as worship and/or idolizing Rozelle over you?"

He showed me, for years, my entire mood would change negatively if we didn't agree on something. I'd mull over the conversation incessantly trying to figure out what I did wrong and how to avoid doing it in the future. Repeatedly, I'd ask the Lord in prayer to change my heart and help me not react to a point where my entire day would be disrupted. This day I got my answer, and I was immediately tasked with ending my misaligned worship of my husband.

He said, "You've placed so much worth on what he thinks about you and how he talks to you, that you don't believe what I've said about you." That stung really bad. I said, "Lord, as a wife, I'm supposed to be pleasing and in agreement with my husband. Isn't that what you say in your word?" He said, "Yes, but not the way you're going about it."

I thought revering my husband meant placing his contentment above me and everyone else.

I thought revering my husband meant placing his contentment above me and everyone else. He began to show me a pattern of thinking I adopted from being misinformed for so many **years**. For example, when the Lord would tell me during prayer that I was loved and adored I'd outwardly say, "I love and adore you too Lord," but I didn't believe Him. I'd immediately start thinking about all the times Rozelle told me things to the contrary and I'd place his opinion of me higher than God's.

In short, I made Rozelle an idol. It didn't matter what God said to me or about me, I believed Rozelle's flawed human perspective of me was more important. Thus, I aimed to change his image of me, and I dismissed God's word and care for me. It was very evident in my everyday life. This warped way of thinking only kept this vicious cycle going in our marriage for years.

Marriage in the kingdom of God doesn't operate like this.

I was emulating what I thought I'd seen done in most of the marriages I admired. Most women would give me advice that supported walking in agreement with Rozelle and revering him. They'd assure me that agreement between us was the catalyst to him hearing from the Lord on his own. I took this advice to heart and at times I was downright disobedient when the Lord gave me directives. Again, I never knew that I, was in fact, making Rozelle an idol and worshiping him.

The Lord said, how you've been conducting yourself for decades is completely in line with the world's system and their definition of marriage. Marriage in the kingdom of God doesn't operate like this.

The second commandment (Exodus 20) in the *Berean Study Bible* says, you shall not make for yourselves an idol of any kind or an image of anything in the heavens above, on the earth beneath, or in the waters below. You shall not bow down to them or worship them; for I, the LORD your God, am a jealous God. This is the first time God refers to Himself as jealous.

Additionally, the Old English definition for bow or bend is to confine with a string or fetter. I was confined and shackled by misinformation that caused me to bend and conform inappropriately under the auspices of "love and reverence." The instructions for wives in Ephesians 5:24 don't mean making our husbands idols resulting in us feeling worthless.

Consequently, I was determined to prove that I wasn't worthless to Rozelle so my actions toward him were cold and calloused and this only enabled his narcissistic personality disorder (NPD). This vicious cycle continued for years.

I learned the importance of knowing the Word of God **for yourself** and not adopting other people's interpretations as face value. I also learned the importance of knowing God's love for you **before** you become married. This foundational knowledge is key to not idolizing another human being over yourself and God.

> **Little did I know then that following what God told me to do would be the catalyst to our healing.**

Another example is when the Lord would ask me to do something specific regarding the children and at times ministry work, and I'd immediately say, "You're going to have to tell him as well because he's not going to believe me and he's going to fight me tooth and nail!" I wanted peace in my home more than what He told me to do. Again, believing that our agreement as a couple supersedes being in right standing with God. This was wrong. God wanted to reveal some dead and diseased areas in our marriage, and I remained in the way of progress. All these decisions were based on idol worship and not knowing the true meaning of the scriptures. Little did I know then that following what God told me to do would be the catalyst to our healing in this area. My obedience to the Lord and following through with his instructions, would've underscored some deep-rooted issues that Rozelle suffered with and brought timely healing.

When we pray and ask the Lord for directions and to be pleasing to Him, He creates and orchestrates opportunities to correct behaviors we <u>think</u> are in alignment with His will.

> **Slowly but surely, I began to devalue concepts and thinking patterns I received about marriage that caused me to choose Rozelle over myself and the Lord.**

It's no different than the wilderness experience from slavery to freedom in the Old Testament. The children of Israel were programmed through slavery and inferiority. Their minds and hearts needed to be reprogrammed by God before any outward behaviors change. God continued to reprogram me until I placed His love and adoration for me first. Slowly but surely, I began to devalue concepts and advice I received about marriage that caused me to choose Rozelle over myself and the Lord.

After I was healed in this area, I readily understood how to identify idol worship not only in my marriage but on many other fronts. It took practice but I was able to clearly identify areas that God's word and declaration of me aided in my daily decisions. I noticed my anxiety went away and I was at total peace.

Most importantly, my healing began to emphasize Rozelle's NPD and he recognized it as a major roadblock that was in direct conflict with God's plan for his life. Rather than excusing his behavior and saying, "That's just me," (as he'd said for years) he started realizing all the deficits and family relationships he damaged and/or dismissed that drew attention to this disorder. He was finally ready to face it and overcome it with God's help.

When God created an opportunity for me to receive His love, properly worship Him, and transform my mindset about how wives should reverence their husbands; it precluded Rozelle's healing from narcissistic personality disorder (NPD.)

Once again, something clicked!

> **This scripture confirms that our ways of thinking and how we conduct ourselves are so deeply rooted within us that we don't know where they stem from.**

The *New Living Translation* of Jeremiah 17:9-10 says the human heart is the most deceitful of all things, and desperately wicked. Who really knows how bad it is? But I, the LORD, search all hearts and examine secret motives. I give all people their due rewards, according to what their actions deserve.

This scripture confirms that our ways of thinking and how we conduct ourselves are so deeply rooted within us that we don't know where they stem from. Our hearts deceive us, and only God can examine them and give us what we **really** need, even when we don't know how desperately we need His intervention. He healed our hearts, and Rozelle and I were rewarded with newfound revelation to change our world and the next generation.

In addition to exposing my wrong view on how wives should reverence their husbands, I studied 1 John 5:21. The *International Standard Version* says, little children keep yourselves from idols. Keep yourself from them by always watching out for them. This is a short but powerful verse. Idols are sneaky. They creep in slowly and silently.

Idols rob us of our physical time and mental peace.

An idol is not always a person, it can be hours of media time (Facebook, Instagram, Twitter, TV shows, Netflix, etc.) that you throw away daily. Idols rob us of our physical time and mental peace. As a result, we spend little to no time in prayer or seeking God about our purpose work. The time we do spend in prayer is usually rehearsed and ritualistic. An idol can be anything we adjust (bend) our lives around that takes our focus from our Creator.

Idols are sneaky but easily identifiable. Look at a full week and monitor the number of hours you spend (outside of working and sleeping) on activities. Count those numbers up and ask yourself:

- How much quality time do I spend on my relationship with the Lord?
- How much quality time do I spend being proactive and preparing for what's forthcoming?

Most of us look around and see that we're exactly like those in our community so we don't look or feel out of place. When inevitable storms arise, it reveals our lack of preparation and we spend tons of time trying to repair what wasn't secure and replacing what was lost in the storm. This cycle can go on for years and years because, again, everyone around us does the same thing. That doesn't make it normal because everyone does it. Idols rob you of the time you should be spending on strengthening and stabilizing yourself for upcoming storms, therefore, we remain in a perpetual cycle of reactionary labor and clean up.

The *New Living Translation* of Isaiah 44:9-10 says how foolish are those who manufacture idols. These prized objects are really worthless. The people who worship idols don't know this, so they are all put to shame. Who but a fool would make his own god—an idol that cannot help him one bit? Idols, as the scripture stated, can't help you one bit. Those hours and hours spent leisurely and on your must-do activities can't assist you in the storm clean up. They were wasted. Then we lament to God and question His love and guidance in our lives when we're totally responsible for our own time and how it's spent.

Please don't be like me and be misinformed for years. Spending quality time in prayer, worship and learning God's word is critical to your personal growth, enlightenment, and stability in storms. Closely monitor your time and be sure you're giving the Creator space to transform your life. It's worth it!

God is more important than anything or anyone He created.

In conclusion, our battle is between worshiping our Creator and not His creation(s). Even if the creation is your spouse, your children, your job, your career, or your time, it's misplaced and/or idol worship. Once more, these "things" can't help you one bit. We must keep our priorities in proper order. God is more important that anyone or anything He created.

I studied to show **myself** approved (2 Timothy 2:15) by God and allowed the Holy Spirit to teach me what I didn't have true knowledge of. Now my worship of God has layers and substance because it's according to His will. It's not merely outward or designated to a particular place or time and it's consistently from my heart. It's based on my relationship with the Lord and not on religious beliefs or rituals.

When we ask God to interfere in our lives, He creates situations that will draw you back to Him and these situations highlight our issues so they can be processed for our betterment.

Jeremiah 31:3 in the *King James Bible* says ...Yea, I have loved thee with an everlasting love: therefore, with lovingkindness have I drawn thee. When we ask God to interfere in our lives, He creates situations that'll draw you back to Him and these situations highlight our issues so they can be processed for our betterment. Are you aware of the situations He's creating to draw you back to Him? Stay alert and witness His lovingkindness.

After Rozelle and I unpacked this newfound revelation, we were both shaking our heads in amazement at how God orchestrated such a perfect breakthrough. Once again, something clicked, and God's timing is impeccable!

Let's pray:

Lord, now that I know better, I'll do better. Holy Spirit show me where the root system of my behavior patterns stems from. More than likely, there's something from my childhood or past that I'm unaware of. Help me to divest from how I'm thinking even if it "appears" to be culturally or spiritually correct. I'll do the soul searching and internal work and not shy away from the truths you reveal to me. Your Word says, there is no condemnation to those in Christ Jesus (Romans 8:1) and I won't receive anything but your love and grace in this transformation of my thinking. Thank you for helping me change the entire course of my relationship with you and my marriage. Most importantly, thank you in advance for the generations I'll change as I live out this new revelation. In Jesus's name, Amen.

Lesson 21

You Married an Entire Generation

The *New King James* version of Matthew 19:5 says, ...and the two **shall** become one flesh.

- Shall is the key word.
- Shall denotes time and a process.
- Shall isn't the same as the word will.
- Shall means <u>you</u> have work to do and a part to play.

It wasn't until year 23 of my marriage that I received a true revelation of this. I was living with my brother in our compound, so our families hung out a lot. One summer, he had the front landscape redesigned and created this beautiful outdoor space for bonfires, dinners, barbeques, and relaxation. The project concluded in October. In the Midwest you have a limited number of days that are over 50 degrees in the fall, so we were excited to have a day warm enough to christen the new space before the next season and he decided to build his first bonfire. My sister (his wife) texted me and invited us to come out and join them.

I knew leaving the argument before he had an opportunity to finish his point would make him angrier and that's what I aimed to do.

I was downstairs arguing with Rozelle when I received her text message. Our heated discussion wasn't going well so I abruptly left the conversation mid-sentence to go join the bonfire outside. I knew leaving the argument before he had an opportunity to finish his point would make him angrier and that's what I aimed to do.

As I left the room, I continued to argue with him in my head. I inwardly shouted obscenities as I opened the door, walked through the living room, down the hallway, around the corner through the dining room, then up the stairs to the main level. I walked through the foyer and put my hand on the front doorknob and opened it. I briefly made eye contact with my sister and immediately heard the Holy Spirit say "No, go back down!" I thought to myself, I know I didn't leave my phone. Again, I heard, "No, go back downstairs to your room!"

So, I gestured to my sister that I'd be right back and turned around. Once I got back inside my room, the Holy Spirit said, "Now repeat everything you said about him as you walked through this house and up the stairs to the front door, but this time put YOUR NAME in front of each sentence!"

Here I was, praying and believing for breakthroughs and for us to become closer, yet I was tearing down my home with my own words.

Of course, I said, "I don't even remember everything..." and He interrupted me and said, "Don't worry I'll remind you."

I re-traced my steps through the house and barely over a whisper, I repeated the lewd and venomous things I said under my breath about

Rozelle. It had so much more impact as I put my name in front of each profane word. So much so, the Holy Spirit said "No, don't whisper. Say it exactly the way you did with all the anger and foulness as you did the first time." I was stunned and embarrassed.

Here I was, praying and believing for breakthroughs and for us to become closer, yet I was tearing down my home with my **own** words.

By the time I reached the front door I was near tears. I heard the Lord say:

- "Do you hear how disrespectful you sound?"
- "Do you see how much your whole disposition changed when you were saying YOUR name?"
- "Do you realize you are cursing **yourself** out when you speak to him that way?"

He said, "Rozelle is you. Everything you see in him, all his faults, failures, weaknesses, issues past and present are all **you**. There's no distinction between the two of you in my eyes."

Then He said, "Now once you get outside this door, you make sure you tell your sister what I just showed you."

We both resolved that very day to "beat" this diagnosis. We were relentless.

Once outside, she noticed my countenance and asked what was wrong. After I explained what just took place, we were both stunned and speechless. Clearly it was a very sober bonfire for the two of us as we really reflected on that admonishment.

I later prayed and asked for forgiveness. At that point, the Lord reminded me of an event in 2001 when Rozelle was diagnosed with hypertension.

For a few months he was having dizzy spells and headaches. It was such a scary time, and we were both really shaken up. When he finally went to see a doctor and had his blood pressure checked, they had to immediately give him medication while he was sitting on the exam room table. The physician came back in the room 30 minutes later and had him lie down on his back to re-take his blood pressure. He told him had he not come in he would've definitely had a stroke. He vehemently told us his abnormal blood pressure was not to be taken lightly. We both resolved that very day to "beat" this diagnosis. We were relentless. Working in the medical field we had access to many physicians and professionals, who gave us sound advice about managing and eventually beating hypertension. We were intentional and put a plan together and we did it! I never saw it as **his** problem or **his** diagnosis. I was in lock step with him and we teamed up and won.

The Lord said, "That is what you must always do. You must come together, strategize and plan for the win. You're on the same team. You married his entire family and he married yours. Most importantly, you married all his hurts, pains, sorrows, shortcomings, and generational curses. He did the same with you."

> **"Most importantly, you married all his hurts, pains, sorrows, shortcomings, and generational curses. He did the same with you."**

He told me, "Stacey you're equipped with everything you need to win right within you. Your generation will win if you see him as yourself, and constantly work on what I reveal about him (yourself) to you." I was taken aback. I couldn't believe that I was outfitted to handle this magnanimous task. I had to ponder that statement over and over.

From that day on, the challenge was to speak life about me (Rozelle). Speak positive about me (Rozelle) and to be consistent in speaking faith until it manifested.

After I committed to continuously speak life, I was trusted to see the playbook that God compiled for us. This playbook addressed Rozelle's past, his family, and the things God wanted us to triumph over in this season and in our lifetime. Our charge included continuous prayer for each other, our families, and an accountability structure.

It was clear to me why the enemy would do <u>anything</u> he could to destroy marriages and families.

It was then revealed that I was also responsible for a whole generation, and my two sons are a part of that generation. Not to mention the 63+ (to date) nieces and nephews that we share together. I was sobered and humbled. It was clear to me why the enemy would do <u>anything</u> he could to destroy marriages and families.

It starts with the divisive mindset that we're programmed to believe we're two different people, when in fact, we are ONE and should function as one. Yes, as I've mentioned in other lessons, we have individual purpose work, but this work falls under the marriage initiative that requires teamwork.

Functioning as one means:

- We see and take on whatever our spouse is and accept the game plan to fight for them as we do for ourselves.
- We pray and ask the Lord to show us how to break our generational curses and win.
- We can be trusted not to throw his/her shortcomings in their face when we get upset.

- We allow the Lord to humble us because the outcome is much greater than our temporary discomfort.

The *Berean Study Bible* version of John 15:12-13 says, this is my commandment that you love one another as I have loved you. Greater love has no one than this, that he lay down his life for his friends. Jesus was speaking about Himself and modeled this wonderful plan. I'm equipped to do the same. I lay down my life for Rozelle as he does for me.

Our society tells us to focus on ourselves in a selfish way in our marriages. As I stated earlier, we have continual teamwork, and it includes our families. It's impossible to dig into your past and correct behaviors as well as prime the next generation for success, without considering both families. It's truly powerful to see families the way God sees them. I was also reminded of the mantra I often recited while attending Straight Gate International Church, "Jesus makes families whole!"

Your family was meticulously constructed by God's hands alone and He didn't make a mistake.

As I articulated in Lesson 1, God chose our parents and siblings, and we choose our friends. This is divine and strategic. However, we've been programmed to look at our family members as competition versus an extension of ourselves. We place more emphasis on cultivating friendships and find it second nature to destroy the family unit God created and chose for you. Your family was meticulously constructed by God's hands alone and He didn't make a mistake.

When we marry, we're stating we're committed to love our spouses unconditionally forever. When two people who received flawed love from their childhoods marry each other, the Lord is the only One who can truly show them how to love each other. This takes time and patience. This is the **shall** process I mentioned in the opening paragraph. One of the biggest fallacies' believers have about marriage is the husband and wife are to become one and, in the process, totally disconnect from their families.

> **One of the biggest misconceptions believers have about marriage is the husband and wife are to become one and, in the process, totally disconnect from their families.**

This isn't God's plan. God's plan is for your marriage to be a platform for the next generation, which includes your whole family and your spouse's whole family. The world teaches the opposite of God's kingdom plan for marriage.

The world teaches:

- That sibling rivalry is commonplace, and we don't have to resolve differences with our siblings.
- To love our friends and keep dissension between our siblings.
- That it's okay to have a disagreement with our siblings or parents and never resolve it.
- To treat our parents with disrespect yet highly respect our friends and co-workers.
- That our friends should be esteemed higher than our family members.

Essentially the world communicates that the very people God chose for us to forever relate to, are totally disposable.

God's love and His structure of the family teaches the opposite of the world and most times we as believers totally miss this major component in our marriages. Again, this is the marriage teamwork initiative I mentioned earlier.

When I married Rozelle, I married his parents, siblings, their spouses, and their children. I married them in love.

I'm invested in their spiritual growth just as I am in his spiritual growth. I make it my business to pray for them and speak life and healing over them always.

This marriage teamwork initiative involves these challenges:

- We challenge each other to forgive swiftly when there are disagreements in our families.
- We challenge each other to look closely at ourselves to find the lesson God is teaching **us** in the disagreements.
- We challenge each other to be eager to listen and very slow to speak (James 1:19).
- We remind each other that our children will model what they see us **do** and our actions speak the true sentiments of our hearts.
- We challenge each other to apologize when we're wrong in family issues and tell our children the lesson(s) we've learned.

In addition to this teamwork initiative with Rozelle, God began to show me His plan for our siblings and how He created us to be forever "knitted together" with them.

He said, "You will never fully be complete without them nor will my plan for your life ever <u>exclude</u> them."

This is what the Lord revealed to me in a dream:

> I saw this beautiful, crocheted blanket that had lots of colors and I saw the blanket being unconnected in heaven and the line of yarn reconnected on Earth. He said, "That's your family. I unconnected you in 1970 and reconnected you to your parents

and siblings on Earth." I was amazed at the meticulous detail and how careful He was as he was knitting us together. I then understood the seriousness of His plan for families. He said, "You'll never fully be complete without them nor will my plan for your life ever exclude them."

I was directed to read the *Berean Study Bible* passage of Genesis 18:18-19 about Abraham and his sons. God said he'll command his children and his household after him to keep the way of the LORD by doing what is right and just, in order that the LORD may bring upon Abraham what He has promised. Abraham was chosen to command his children and his household after him to keep the way of the Lord.

Let's expand on "command" and the "way of the Lord" because these two are prerequisites to receive what was promised. After I further researched, I found that command meant by parental authority as well as by personal example. And the way of the Lord is to do righteously by all people, to be moral, intelligent and harmonize his life with Divine Law.

> **You can start by making the commitment to pray for your family, and your spouses' family and committing to speak life over them at all times.**

Parental authority and by personal example are intense. Who better to model this behavior but married couples that hold each other accountable to their families that God knitted them together with. As I cited earlier in the lesson, Jesus's love was displayed by laying down His life for us and we can do the same by adjusting how we view His family structure. You can start by making the commitment to pray for your family, and your spouses' family and committing to speak life over them at all times.

God's love has the power to transform any situation and anyone. All it takes is a willing heart. I pray you have a willing heart to remain committed to your pledge and remind yourself what was spoken to Sarah in Genesis 18:14, "Is there anything too hard for the Lord?"

You married your spouse. You are him/her. Your families are connected in love therefore, you have an entire generation that's awaiting your obedience. Yes, you married an entire generation.

Let's pray:

Lord, I thank you for the assignment you placed in me to become one with my spouse. I'm well prepared and able to finish this work. I won't divide my marriage with my limited thinking and worldly perception of how a couple relates to each other, instead I choose to see us as the same person. I'll care for my spouse as myself. Lord, I also accept the assignment of establishing a generation from my marriage by praying and speaking life to our siblings. You made the decision to knit us together and didn't leave that choice up to me. Help me connect to my siblings and rid of rivalry and dissension. Lastly Lord, I'll earnestly pray for my spouse's siblings and their families. I won't divide our family unit and give way for competition and discord. I understand that I'm not complete or whole without the input of all these individuals. In this process you'll be glorified Father, and nothing is too difficult for you. Absolutely nothing. In Jesus's name, Amen.

Long Suffering vs. Suffering Long

As I've cited in other chapters, we're a product of our childhood experiences, but we're never to accept the negative experiences as the end. They're only the beginning.

We had a major breakthrough in March of 2019. It was a generational curse that we faced, fought, and conquered. I remember celebrating our 25th wedding anniversary the previous March and saying, "Lord, Abraham received his promise 25 years after you declared it. I'm expecting to receive our promise this year." Little did I know then that the root to our promise extended back 40 years.

Rozelle was raised in an environment where alcoholism and drug abuse were prevalent. He remembers his parents deciding to divorce after a few tumultuous years of marriage. As the oldest child, he recalled the arguments and dysfunction. He noticed he'd adopted a coping mechanism his mother used. It was stemmed from her pain, hurt, rejection, and abandonment from her childhood. He recollected her saying on occasion, "Once you've hurt me, you'll never hurt me again!"

Of course, these are things you're unaware of when you're dating someone, but as time passes, you see the behaviors surface. I'd always say, "Babe, you're mean! You judge people and act as if you're without any fault." I didn't know at the time, the root of these behaviors stemmed from his childhood hurts and pains. He witnessed his parents exhibit this behavior and thought it was normal and justifiable.

> **When your primary relationship (parents) shows you how to handle conflict, you deem it as normal and acceptable, even if it's not.**

When your primary relationship (parents) shows you how to handle conflict, you deem it as normal and acceptable, even if it's not. I learned from our therapy sessions the impact of parenting, and how our primary relationships set the foundation for our marriages. Whether positive or negative, that foundation is what we're built on and it's our responsibility to correct the damages with God's help.

Now, I was raised in a household where loud arguing and hurling hurtful words was commonplace, but we were commanded not to hold grudges. My mother didn't allow it. She'd say, "This house is too small, and we're too close in quarters to be mad and hold grudges in here." She'd also say, "You have nothing to be mad or sad about so let it go and get glad... like, right now!" Consequently, my siblings and I learned this as normal behavior when it was abnormal as well. Essentially, we mastered the art of masking our anger, while outwardly saying we weren't holding on to it. We'd unleash that fury of anger on those outside of our home for the smallest of things when they made us upset.

You can only imagine coming from my home where we loved each other, fought with our words, made up swiftly, and couldn't hold grudges, connected with Rozelle's childhood coping mechanisms; it was a recipe for confusion and disaster. When I'd argue with Rozelle and attempt to make up, so we could go on with our day, he'd be livid and say, "No, it doesn't work like that. I don't want to talk or be around you!" I'd say, "Wait a minute. Are you still holding on to that? Why can't we talk about it and move on?"

Over time, I grew bitter with being judged and feeling like he purposely didn't communicate because he knew I wanted to. Well, this continued for years and we learned to manage with this type of deformed communication. It got worse and worse. After a while, I noticed we were growing as friends, but our husband/wife roles weren't flourishing because true communication is necessary for <u>healthy</u> growth.

For years, I had the strength and energy to argue and manipulate the relationship to get the outcome I wanted, and he'd do the same. As the years progressed, the new order became discussing only what was incredibly important and letting the other things fall through the cracks. By the time we had children and focused on raising them, some of those hot button items seem to disappear altogether, or so I thought.

Communication precedes trust and trust produces intimacy. Prior to getting married, we hadn't learned as single individuals to be truly intimate with the Lord. Consequently, communicating with each other and trusting each other was again, skewed at its best. When you're convinced, you're correct and your spouse isn't, it delays growth and progress. Then we lie to ourselves and believe our delay isn't visible to others around us and that it's not worth the temporary pain for permanent growth. That's self-deception at its finest.

As time progressed, we noticed our dysfunctional coping mechanisms manifest in our children, that's when I knew we could no longer ignore them.

As time progressed, we noticed our dysfunctional coping mechanisms manifest in our children, that's when I knew we could no longer ignore them. I asked the Lord to show me the root of our issues. While there was love in our home and we could see God's hand over our lives, this issue was becoming more and more disruptive. It seemed to grow and take over our lives. Now, here we are with young adults and in ministry full time, and I knew something wasn't quite right.

This is where prayer and seeking God is imperative. The Lord will create and orchestrate opportunities to defeat dysfunctional behaviors, no matter how deep the root system is.

Longsuffering is a fruit of the Spirit. Suffering long is a fruit of the flesh.

The Lord was longsuffering with us as we continued to "suffer long." Sometimes, we're not aware of our issues, but we continually see the harm it's causing in our lives. Blindly, we attempt to address them without the guidance of the only person equipped to do so. On the other hand, there are cases when we are very much aware of our issues but refuse to do the work to eliminate them. The latter is suffering long.

Let's compare the two. Longsuffering is a fruit of the Spirit. Suffering long is a fruit of the flesh.

When I researched longsuffering, I found that it's:

1	Having or showing patience despite troubles you caused.
2	Having or showing patience despite troubles, especially those caused by other people.
3	Patiently enduring through lasting offense or hardship.

The patience that we abundantly **receive** from the Lord for our issues and shortcomings is the patience we're equipped to give to others. Yes, it's that simple. I've been a recipient of God's patience therefore I can give God's patience to others. I've stated in other lessons, He never requires from us, something He hasn't freely given to us.

This patience/longsuffering is also known as purposeful time. Purposeful time just like what's necessary for the wine-making process.

For instance, I learned the importance of purposeful time when I visited a winery in Florence, Italy. They referred to the passing of purposeful time as aging. In wine production, grapes are harvested and crushed for their juice, and aging is mandatory. Aging is significant because each day something purposeful is happening to enhance the quality of the wine, and each passing year affects the worth of wine. Aging is a crucial step that can't be rushed. Aging is also defined as maturity.

The *New International Version* of Ephesians 4:13 says until we all reach unity in the faith and in the knowledge of the Son of God and become mature, attaining to the whole measure of the fullness of Christ.

You're not responsible for anyone's maturity in Christ, but your own.

You're not responsible for anyone's maturity in Christ, but your own. When we put others on a "clock," which is man's measurement of time, rather than submit to God's purposeful time, we're essentially trying to play the role of God. Regardless to the mere passing of time, there's a purpose for each day and each season for all of us.

Therefore, longsuffering has components of:

- Patience
- Purposeful time
- Aging
- Enhancement
- Quality
- Worth
- Maturity

These components are what the Lord has freely given to us, so, when we're cultivating this fruit of the Spirit in our lives, it has layers and innumerable benefits.

The Lord loves us and only has good plans for us. He was longsuffering towards us because He knew we'd overcome by aging and that we were worth the process. He's not bound by man's measurement of time. Our communication matured and our dysfunctional roots were slowly eradicated.

Now let's take a deep dive into "suffering long." Again, suffering long is not a fruit of the Spirit, but of the flesh.

1	It's taking matters into your own hands without careful consideration of the consequences.
2	It's attempting to fight in your own strength and using your own knowledge.
3	It's thinking you don't need the Lord to get involved because "you got this."
4	It's accepting what your childhood consisted of as the end without hope for change.

5	It's believing your parents impact on you is greater than God's.
6	It's rooted in pride.

Proverbs 3:6 admonishes us to acknowledge Him in all our ways and He'll direct our paths. The keyword is **ways**. That means ways of thinking you've incorporated into your life that you trust and heavily rely on.

If you've heard the expression, "You only want to do things your way?" Well, this implies that what you're doing is effective and works for you. The danger in this is never acknowledging God to see if your way is still applicable for this day or season. Our ways must be updated and sometimes eliminated to match what's forthcoming in our lives.

We often refer to the elderly as "stuck in their ways" and this is a negative connotation. It signifies someone who isn't open to change and that's dangerous. When you're not open to change, you'll soon realize you're left behind while others are progressing. Suffering long is evidenced in the lives of those who are stuck in their ways or only do things their way.

I suffered long with distorted communication in my marriage because I didn't acknowledge the Lord and His plan for freedom in this area. I didn't ask for His direction and illumination. I blamed Rozelle for years and felt when he changed, it would change for all of us. I didn't see it as an issue that I was responsible for. I didn't ask either because I was entrenched in my way. My stance was "God will tell me what my part is and if He hasn't, clearly it's not me." I was dead wrong. I was blinded by pride. Pride closed my ability to hear clearly, and I <u>didn't</u> pray about it because I'd convinced myself it wasn't my issue.

That, in itself is the issue. I was set in my way of communicating. I had a major role in our deformed communication and our merciful Lord kept creating **opportunities** for me to see this.

The *Pulpit Commentary* for Proverbs 3:6 states, "Acknowledging God also implies that we first ascertain whether what we are about to take in hand is in accordance with his precepts (principles), and then look for his direction and illumination..."

Now ask yourself:

- Is your way the best?
- Is your way still relevant for today?
- Is your way in line with Godly principles?
- Is your way yielding fruit or causing stagnation?

Based on your answers, **you can** determine for yourself if you will suffer long.

To receive direction and illumination, you must first absolve yourself of pride and unbelief. Let's refer to the Children of Israel and how they suffered long in the wilderness because of their pride and unbelief.

The temporary wilderness isn't designed for permanent placement. It's designed for training and education.

You recall their story, after 430 years of suffering under Egyptian rule, they were miraculously freed by God Himself. They were removed from their geographical place of slavery and suffering then placed in a new temporary location for their reprogramming, growth, and development. The temporary wilderness isn't designed for permanent placement. It's designed for training and education. They were physically removed from slavery and now slavery had to be removed from their (mind) hearts.

Their pride and unbelief caused those who weren't willing to release their slave mentality, to die and never attain true freedom. The age of accountability that God determined was 20 years old, which is military fighting age. Everyone over the age of 20 died a slave although they were "free."

However, God in His love and omniscience, didn't punish their children. He allowed them to grow, witness the error of their parents, and decide on their own. This is where we as adults, must be careful not to lament and magnify the suffering of our childhoods over the solutions and freedom God provides for us to receive. We no longer physically reside in our parents' homes just as the Children of Egypt no longer lived in Egypt.

They didn't look to God for direction and illumination, and it costs them long undue suffering and their lives. They decided to cling to their slave mentality versus overcoming it and obtaining all the benefits, rights, and privileges of freedom.

> **More than likely, the Lord will speak to you through your family members and those you're quick to dismiss because they "know" you.**

Our opportunities come in many forms. He didn't always speak directly to me about my struggles and issues, He'd speak to me through other people. More than likely, the Lord will speak to you through your family members and those you're quick to dismiss because they "know" you. Subsequently, you judge the messenger rather than adhere to the message. This is a clear sign of pride and immaturity and it exacerbates suffering long.

After finally saying, "Ugh, how long are we going to have to deal with this Lord? I now see the pain it's causing our children, Jesus help!" He did. He began by directing us to our individual "slavery" mentalities from our childhoods so we could defeat them, then He illuminated our path to freedom.

In addition to healing our communication, we've faced, fought, and conquered:

- Anger
- Abuse
- Addiction
- False self-image
- Low self esteem
- Narcissistic personality disorder
- Poverty mentality

It was consistent, daily work that was necessary for our reprogramming. We learned that the errors from our parents weren't our fault, however, making the decision to fight and defeat those errors was totally our choice. I knew if we didn't choose to heed the time and overcome them, they'd lead to death and manifest in our children.

> **The hardest part after conquering is maintaining victory. The processes we installed to remain victorious are the keys to continual success.**

The hardest part after conquering is maintaining victory. The processes we installed to remain victorious are the keys to continual success. The Holy Spirit is the Master of plans and solutions, it's impossible to achieve this without His help. Be it, reading the word, prayer, therapy, counseling, confessions, keeping proper company and conversations; none of these work without fasting. Fasting is the partner to all the aforementioned. Make fasting and consecration a lifestyle and you'll see continual benefits.

We ended the cycle of suffering long. We stopped taking matters into our own hands through pride and unbelief. We acknowledged the Lord, and He directed each step of our path to this remarkable outcome!

Let's pray:

Lord, I don't want to suffer long. I want to seek your face and acknowledge you about the ways I'm confident I already know. I thank you Holy Spirit for helping me identify these areas and clear pride from my life. Pride robs and strips me of opportunities to grow and Lord, you hate pride. I thank you that I'm manifesting the fruit of the Spirit in my life which includes longsuffering. Lord, I'm a recipient of your longsuffering therefore I'm charged to exhibit longsuffering to those in need. I don't want to be like the Children of Israel and choose to rely on what I know, rather than what you want to teach me. You're God and you're all-knowing. Holy Spirit search those hidden chambers of my heart and expose all areas that don't bring glory to the Father. I won't be embarrassed, nor will I dismiss the **opportunities** and individuals you choose for orchestrating my healing and freedom. I thank you in advance for major breakthroughs that will encourage someone else to give their slavery mentality over to you. Thank you for loving me perfectly Lord. I love you.

Your Marriage Has Its Own Fingerprints, Teeth, and Vocal Cords

We have an inherent longing to belong and identify with other human beings. However, in our world, it's a constant fight to be unique and different. I know God placed that longing within us, but not for the purpose of us losing our identity in Him.

To date, there are approximately 7.7 billion people on Earth and each one of us has our own unique identifiers that God gave us. Our fingerprints aren't like any other person on Earth. Likewise, our teeth aren't like any other person on Earth and most notably, our vocal cords are one of a kind.

Those facts are mind blowing to me, so I researched to find out more. I found that the faint lines you see on your fingers and toes were completely formed by the time you were six months old in the womb, which is three months **before** you were born! Scientists agree that fingerprints begin to develop around the 10th week of pregnancy, but they aren't certain of the precise process that creates them. Of course, they don't know the precise process, clearly God knows and some knowledge He chooses <u>not</u> to make known to man. I love that about God, He constantly bewilders human knowledge of science with His omniscience.

> **I love that about God, He constantly bewilders human knowledge of science with His omniscience.**

Your teeth and your fingerprints are incorporated into our world's identification system because they're uniquely yours. Therefore, dental records are sometimes used to identify human remains and fingerprints are used in law enforcement for collecting evidence. Even identical twins don't have identical teeth or fingerprints. In fact, your tongue also has a unique "tongue print" that no one else on the Earth has. Once more, proof that God wanted you to be here, so rest assured, you were specifically created for a GREAT purpose.

Of all our God-given identifiers, I was most fascinated by the vocal cords. Each of us have a unique voice because so many factors work together to produce our voices. Your voice starts down in your lungs, where air is exhaled to create an airstream in the trachea and across the larynx, which is often called the voice box.

While reading an article on Wonderopolis.org, titled, Why Does Everyone Have a Unique Voice (2015), I learned more on the subject. The article stated,

> *"...stretched horizontally across your larynx are vocal folds, which are also known as vocal cords. The pitch of your voice is largely determined by the length and tension of your vocal cords. By themselves, the vocal cords produce just a buzzing sound. The parts of your body between the vocal cords and the outside world, such as the throat, nose, and mouth, act as a resonating chamber to turn those buzzing sounds into your unique human voice. There are many different parts of the body involved in producing your voice. Each of those parts is unique in*

each person. Moreover, those parts can change over the years and even from day to day, so your voice itself can change over time and even day to day!"

Wow, God knows the sound of every person on this Earth and even as we're growing, He still knows our distinct voices. That's bewildering! I've witnessed my voice change several times in a day from the time I woke up until I went to bed. Especially if I taught a lot of classes, I could hear a distinct difference by the end of the day. The amount of care, consideration and thought that He put into creating us is overwhelming.

Therefore, your marriage has its OWN fingerprints, teeth, and vocal cords!

Concurrently, God created you, your spouse and He created marriage. Therefore, your marriage has its OWN fingerprints, teeth, and vocal cords!

I love documentaries and anything that draws attention to nature. When my son Austin was younger, we'd binge-watch the National Geographic and Discovery channels. I remember seeing an episode about different insects and the types of flowers they pollinate. I learned that certain insects and bees can only see certain colors. This is done to ensure there's always an equity of resources and food. Specific insects can only see orange or yellow, while others can only see red or pink. This is incredible to me and I asked the Lord is it the same for humans?

He said, "Yes, I programmed and tuned your ears to hear certain people. You're also attracted by what your eyes are programmed to see." The **see** He was referring to is the same visual connotation to insects and flowers.

I was intrigued and immediately thought about Rozelle and me. It's true as I have my favorite book authors and when I read their materials it seems as if I equate to them and easily comprehend what they're conveying. Rozelle has a distinct library of his favorite book authors also, and they appeal to him perfectly. Additionally, I have a library of my favorite speakers, podcasts, and YouTube videos based on who draws to me. That doesn't mean those who Rozelle listens to aren't valuable; my ears are just tuned to hear and understand others. I'm always astonished even within the body of Christ, how we're attracted to different types of speakers, teachers, and preachers. It's based on how God tuned your ears and programmed your eyes.

Now, let's link this to marriage. We should be diligent in listening for those that agree with what God said about marriage first. Then we must listen to and look for those couples that have the same "colors and sounds" we're programmed to see and hear. This is key to the success of your marriage.

As I've expressed in other lessons, when we get married, we become one over time. Becoming denotes it's a daily ongoing process. Listening and seeing is a daily process as well. It should never be forsaken. After hearing so many people give good advice and unsolicited bad advice to me about marriage, I questioned why the Lord said there's safety in a multitude of counsel. (Proverbs 11:4) I decided to research it.

I said, "Lord, you're the Wonderful Counselor, I need answers." The first answer I received was, "Listen closely to what the person is saying and see if that answer resonates with what I said to you about **your** marriage."

For example, I remember going to visit a longtime family friend who moved to another state. My sisters and I were vacationing in her new hometown and connected with her for a visit. We had the best time talking and catching up over lunch. She and her husband had recently celebrated their 20th wedding anniversary, so I asked her, "Tell me the secret, how do I make it to 20 years?" She chuckled and said, "Girl, don't ask any questions and take separate vacations!"

I didn't find the advice funny and wondered if it was just "over my head" at the time. Honestly, I was bewildered. Here I was in year three of my marriage and struggling to keep my head above water, and one of the women I admired so much had <u>that</u> advice? I remember going outside to the pool area and sitting quietly. I was so disappointed and confused. Unquestionably, this wasn't sound advice and something I wanted to adopt. I said, "Lord that sounds like division and avoidance, I don't want that, especially after 20 years." At that moment I distinctly heard the Lord say, "Well, what did I say to you about YOUR marriage Stacey?"

I said, "Lord you said my marriage will be an example for others in my generation to emulate." For the remainder of the vacation, I rehearsed that statement inwardly and just focused on enjoying myself.

After my vacation, I did more research on Proverbs 11:4 which says there is safety in a multitude of counsel. I found a few translations and cross-references that resonated with me.

1	*New Living Translation* version of Proverbs 20:18 says **plans** succeed through good counsel; don't go to war without wise advice.
2	*Contemporary English Version* of Proverbs 11:14 says a **city** without wise leaders will end up in ruin; a city with many wise leaders will be kept safe.
3	*Douay Rheims Bible* version of Proverbs 15:22 says **designs** are brought to nothing where there is no counsel: but where there are many counselors, they are established.
4	*Berean Study Bible* version of Proverbs 24:6 says only with sound guidance should you **wage war**, and victory lies in a multitude of counselors.

I highlighted the above scriptures because in marriage you'll be faced with:

- Planning
- Building a city/family
- Designing
- Fighting a War

You won't succeed if you don't know what God said to you about your unique marriage. It's your responsibility to understand and appreciate what your unique traits are for your marriage. Left to the wisdom of improper "counselors," your planning, building, designing, and fighting will be futile. Once you know what He said, ask the Lord to tune your ears to be able to **hear** what good counsel and sound guidance is from those around you. I also asked the Lord to help me **see** the marriages around me that imitate what He designed.

> **Left to the wisdom of improper "counselors," your planning, building, designing, and fighting will be futile.**

You see, this couple was financially sound, they loved their children, and were the nicest people ever. Even with these noteworthy traits, they didn't define marriage the way God had for Rozelle and me. Even in year three, I understood a marriage must be built, and it wasn't always going to be sunshine, but I felt that after 20 years, she would've given me something of more substance to glean from.

In hindsight, I would've done better to have gone further and solicited advice about my career path and/or relocation. They were well-versed in business and successful in these areas. The conversation didn't have to end because I disagreed with her perspective on marriage. I know people who I love dearly that don't fight hard to reach their goals in marriage, I still connect with them, but I don't discuss marriage. I find other commonalities and like goals that we share.

So, while marriages have their own fingerprints, teeth, and vocal cords we're still connected and grouped by other commonalities much like the insect community. I was tasked with finding my community, realizing some family and/or longtime friends, aren't automatically included.

To date, I've been married 28 years and now I'm aware that somewhere along their journey, that couple didn't make one or two of the bullet points above a consistent priority within their marriage. Perhaps it became unbearable at times and it was easier to settle for "good enough." Either way, I was charged by the Lord early on in my marriage to fight and not settle.

Either way, I was charged by the Lord early on in my marriage to fight and not settle.

It was extremely difficult at times, and I made a lot of mistakes, but the Lord would remind me of this charge. Even when I struggled to remain focused, God gave me the strength.

I realize no marriage is perfect, but our Creator is. I'm incredibly careful to reach out to certain couples for specific advice. For instance, I call a completely different couple about financial advice than I call for advice on parenting. Similarly, I reach out to another couple for health and wellness, yet don't seek their advice on family relationships. I learned over time that my "multitude of counsel" consist of specific people for specific reasons, and with them altogether, I win.

What's ironic is, if you witnessed our craziness during those early years, you'd never solicit us for <u>any</u> type of advice in any area. The lesson is, we only grow if we make the daily choice to and accomplish the necessary work that follows.

I'm extremely knowledgeable about what God said to me about Rozelle and my family. I hold that word near and dear to my heart and I don't deviate from it. We're unique and one of a kind and there are certain people who may not understand us. We don't persist and pursue to be understood by those outside of our unique marriage community; we still have a purpose and mission to fulfill and a "well-done" to receive.

There's only one Rozelle F. and Stacey L. Prater White and there's only one (fill in your names) _____.

We're **ALL** extraordinarily special to God!

Consult the Wonderful Counselor about everything and He'll connect you to the community you're tuned to **hear** and those you're created to **see**.

Let's pray:

Lord, your love for me, my spouse and our marriage are mind-blowing. The care and attention you created us with shows how much you wanted us to know that we **matter** to you! Thank you.

Help me to walk in my uniqueness. Support me in appreciating every specific trait. I love that you know my voice and hear me when I talk to you. I love that you tuned my ears to hear your voice and at times, confirm it through others I see and hear. Never again will I compare myself to someone else. Never again will I compare my marriage to anyone else's because that diminishes your meticulous handiwork. By faith, I speak life to my uniquely created marriage, and we'll fulfill the mission, purpose, and work you designed for us. In Jesus's name, Amen.

Lesson 18

Same Year, Make and Model but different VIN Numbers

I love Hondas, specifically Honda Accords. I was blessed with one by a dear couple years ago and at the time it had 190K miles on it. It was in pristine condition and had been well-maintained by a retired Honda mechanic its "whole life." I acquired it and kept the same precedent.

We were blessed to be a blessing and gave it to a sweet college student some years later, at that time it had 325K miles on it. That car held a special place in our hearts because it was manufactured the same year we were married, in 1993.

In August of 2010, I was living in Franklin, Tennessee and needed a new car. One day after work, I went to the nearby Honda dealership with my son Andrew. It was at least 95 degrees that day, so I stayed inside the air-conditioned showroom and told him, "Go out to the lot and pick your new car." He looked at me with a weird expression. I said, "Yeah, in about eight years or so you'll be driving, and it'll still be running, so go pick out **your** car." He smiled at me, left to peruse the lot, and chose the silver 2010 sedan. We name him DJ.

A week or so later, my good friend and neighbor Heather was also shopping for a new car. She inquired about DJ and asked how I liked this newer model. I told her "he" was perfect and a great investment as I didn't like to purchase cars often. I told her I planned to drive DJ until he literally stopped running.

She went to the same dealership and purchased one as well. She was looking for another color, but it would have to be special ordered, and she didn't want to wait, so she got a silver one as well. It was cool seeing each other around the vicinity and waving as we passed by driving our new Hondas.

I lived in Tennessee for another two years before we relocated back home to Michigan. Heather and her family lived in Tennessee for another five years before moving to Arizona. So here we were with the exact same vehicle (year, make, model, color), however, we retained two **different** VIN numbers.

When I researched automobile VIN numbers, I found an article that stated:

> *The car's vehicle identification number (VIN) is the identifying code for a SPECIFIC automobile. The VIN serves as the car's fingerprint, as no two vehicles in operation have the same VIN. A VIN is composed of 17 characters (digits and capital letters) that act as a unique identifier for the vehicle. In the 10th position, you'll see a letter indicating the model year.* Montoya, Ronald, "VIN Lookup: How to Decode Your Vin" (2019)

The definition of care is serious attention or consideration applied to doing something correctly or to avoid damage or risk.

Regardless to the similarities we shared, our purposes and plans for our vehicles were completely different. How I cared for my vehicle would determine its longevity and quality of life. The same is true of my marriage; regardless to the similarities I share with others in my village, how I "care" for it determines its longevity and quality of life.

The definition of **care** is serious attention or consideration applied to doing something correctly or to avoid damage or risk. I believe you should meticulously care for your vehicle as its essential to everyday life and poses major challenges when it's not in operation. Rozelle would tease me when he'd be driving our '93 Honda and I'd say, "Babe, do you hear that? I hear a noise when you hit the brakes." He would say, "Babe ain't nothing wrong with this car, that was just something on the road." I would still ask him to take the car to the service department just in case something was really wrong. Sometimes, there wasn't anything of concern and other times, albeit minor, there was. This detailed level of care attributed to our '93 Honda surpassing 325K miles.

I paid the same serious attention to every aspect of DJ and still do.

When I was a young wife, I wasn't **careful** at all. I didn't pay serious attention to my actions in my marriage and avoiding damage or risk wasn't a priority. I'd get so frustrated trying to figure things out on my own. Sometimes, I had to repair and clean up all the things I did on my own before getting the real answers. It was time consuming and counterproductive.

For example, I love to clean. It's weird but I do the most thinking and problem solving when I'm cleaning. I also appreciate a neat and organized environment because it helps me stay calm. As luck would have it, Rozelle was the opposite when we were newlyweds. He didn't mind a little "organized chaos." When he was pursuing his MBA, while he went to his 4-hour Saturday classes, I'd clean our townhome from top to bottom and do all the laundry. As I'm cleaning, I'm cussing Rozelle out in my head for having to clean and organize all his stuff he left around the house during the week.

One Saturday, he walked in from school and put his book bag on the floor that I just mopped and waxed, and he tracked dirt across the floor. When I saw the floor, I started screaming to the top of my lungs and accused him of doing it on purpose! He looked at me like I was crazy and wanted to know why his mistake warranted that level of a response? I said, "I told you a million times that the floor takes 45 minutes to dry and you walked on it anyway just to spite me!" He calmly said, "Umm, what are you talking about? I left the house at 7 o'clock this morning and I haven't had one conversation with you all day until now."

In reality, I had multiple conversations with him in my head about keeping the house clean and how much I loathed cleaning up after him. He wasn't even present, and I was livid that he didn't regard what "I said" and all my hard work.

Additionally, he wasn't even thinking about the floor because he was preoccupied with a grade he received on a team project earlier. Rozelle was a perfectionist when it came to his academics and earned straight A's, so the thought of having to work with a team for a project didn't sit well with him at all. His focus was on the team grade they'd received, and he never looked down at the floor when he walked in.

I stood there and pondered to myself, "Well, who was I **talking** to if you weren't here?"

It became apparent at that moment that I was judging him and treating him as if he blatantly ignored me, and he was nowhere around. I had to apologize. Not only for this scenario, but for every week prior that I treated him horribly after cleaning the house and he'd come home not knowing why I had such a bad attitude.

I also had to learn to communicate effectively to avoid "damage or risk" as the definition indicates.

That Saturday, I got real answers to a problem that I unknowingly created in my early days of marriage. I obligated to be mindful of my demeaning words and nasty attitude I entertained in my head. Now that it was exposed, I needed to be more **careful**. I didn't have an excuse not to give serious attention and consideration to my part in disagreements. I also had to learn to communicate effectively to avoid "damage or risk" as the definition indicates. That week we established a home maintenance and cleaning structure that we still use to this day.

In addition to caring for our vehicles, Heather and my driving patterns, car insurance rates and purposes for our vehicles were vastly different. Michigan is in the Midwest and our lake effect snow; bone chilling cold, and sub-below temps are not for the weak! From December to March, our average temperatures remain below freezing all day long. Arizona averages one hundred days a year with temperatures over 100 degrees. Thus, our geographical locations denoted two totally different maintenance plans and costs. Not to mention the car insurance rates in Michigan are the highest in the entire country. How we maintained our vehicles to keep operating effectively in two opposing climates were entirely different.

The definition of maintenance is the process of preserving someone or something, or the state of being maintained.

The definition of **maintenance** is the process of preserving someone or something, or the state of being maintained. I've only taken my car to Honda service departments for maintenance. I'm aware of the extra costs, but it's worth it to me to have one record and the maker of the vehicle to service it. To date, DJ is over ten years old and is in very good condition. We follow the suggested manufacturer's maintenance plan to the letter and it's working for us.

One day, I was lamenting to the Lord about my marriage and why Rozelle and I were so different from other couples who looked like us. Meaning they worshiped our God, had similar morals, values and cultural backgrounds and we were in the same geographical location.

> **He answered, "Your maintenance plan is different based on your purpose and what I've called you to do.**

He answered, "Your maintenance plan is different based on your purpose and what I've called you to do. Those other couples have different purposes and callings. It's not the same as yours." It was so simple and made a lot of sense and that comforted me. Just as the other Honda owners in my area are good resources should I have general questions, but the purposes for our cars vary greatly. The purpose for my Honda from the day I purchased it was longevity. The primary purpose for my marriage was the same. Years ago, I did some researched, and Honda has an award-winning reputation for manufacturing cars that last a long time, when given the proper care. Consequently, we still must do our part to ensure the purpose of longevity is fulfilled. The couples in my community have the same purpose of longevity in their marriages, however; they still must achieve their part to ensure it.

Regardless to how the outer body of Heather and my Hondas looked, it wasn't a true depiction of what was going on the inside the car and more importantly under the hood. Most service departments can run a 45-point inspection to evaluate the health of your vehicle and the results are completely different for each vehicle. In comparison, our "45-point marriage inspection from the Lord" is different from the next couple.

I used this very detailed story to reinforce one central point: I learned not to compare. Comparison is strictly visual. What is visually seen isn't the whole truth. All too often social media intensifies this point. What people post isn't the "inspection results", just the outer view, so comparing is pointless.

I don't feel the pressure to make my marriage look like others.

Rozelle and I are becoming one. This process is daily and lifelong. I couldn't afford to compare, and I had to stay connected to the creator and manufacturer of our "engine and VIN number." Now that I'm settled in our calling and declaration of longevity, I don't feel the pressure to make my marriage look like others. I rely on the reality that while we have similarities, we're totally different in God's eyes, and we must to look to Him for direction and maintenance. The manufacturer of marriage created an owner's manual for Rozelle and me, and if we followed exactly what He explained in our manual, at the proper time intervals, we'd be successful. That's what we do.

The Lord lead me on the path to success for my marriage and told me to keep my nose in my own one-of-a-kind owner's manual because He's the key to longevity. I began to see major changes for the better after I adopted this mindset. I took pride in our exclusivity because it's only one Rozelle and Stacey in the whole world! My goal became maximizing my marriage to last for years and years and increase in worth just like vintage cars.

- What makes a car vintage is standing the test of time.
- What makes a vintage car valuable is there maintenance records and original parts.
- What makes a vintage car worth so much is no current cars look like them and they inspire those who are aficionados in that particular manufacturer, make and model.

We want to inspire and increase the value of marriage God's way, while promoting unique individuality.

Our God specializes in individuality. We want to inspire and increase the value of marriage God's way, while promoting unique individuality.

God's Word Translation of Jeremiah 1:5 says, before I formed you in the womb, I knew you. Before you were born, I set you apart for my holy purpose. I appointed you to be a prophet to the nations. The *New International Version* of Psalm 139:16 says, your eyes saw my unformed body; all my days were written in Your book and ordained for me before one of them came to be.

You and your spouse were known by God before you became a couple. You both have a holy purpose. God has a set number of days for each of your lives so maximize each day by fulfilling your purpose. Never forget the love, attention, and meticulous detail that went into creating you and your spouse. Above all, never make light of the identifier (VIN) that ONLY the two of you share.

The Creator also knows what will comprise your children's marriages so you should speak life to them now. Yes, DJ is still running and when Andrew was in drivers training, he drove DJ for his road test before joining the United States Air Force. Our declaration of longevity for him via proper and timely maintenance is still the goal.

I pray that my children:

1	Enter their marriages with a purpose of longevity and vintage status as the goal.
2	See the benefit of investing in their marriages and caring for their spouses.

3	Have the Only certified, master mechanic of marriage inspect their marriages.
4	Seek His service department when they need maintenance because He only uses parts that are created for them, and He keeps impeccable records.

I pray you consider the same goals for your children as the next generation benefits from our examples.

Let's pray:

Lord, help me come to know the purpose for **my** marriage although I'm surrounded by so many others with visible likenesses. I'll consult my current community of marriages for support and general information but not for "inspection." Only you know what my spouse and I were created for and the goal for our marriage. You designed marriage for longevity and to increase in value. You also designed marriage to inspire the next generation and for the foundation of Godly families. Godly families support communities and advance your kingdom. Help me Holy Spirit, to understand the magnitude and weight of our marriage assignment, and to cautiously follow your one-of-a-kind maintenance and care plan. In Jesus's name, Amen.

Lesson 17

Love Is Displayed Through Servanthood

*T*his is a lifelong lesson that I didn't fully understand until year 25 of my marriage. It requires consistent effort and humility. Often, we encumber our growth because we refuse to prefer others over ourselves. We're bombarded through society and media that displays the opposite of this Godly concept. This lesson is designed to reprogram your thinking and prepare you for explosive growth, with results only God can give!

- Do you believe you're capable of enduring pain?
- Do you believe God knows exactly how you feel when you're in pain or have been hurt by someone?
- Do you believe you can refrain from retaliation?
- Do you believe that allowing Him to take control means the hurt and pain cease and everyone is made whole?

We'll start by defining what servanthood is from a **biblical** perspective. Keep in mind throughout this lesson the words servanthood and preference are synonymous. Next, I'll outline and demonstrate as a spouse, that you committed to a walk of love when you got married. This love is fueled by acts of servanthood.

According to an article by Dr. Walt Larimore (The High Calling of Servanthood, 2020), biblical servanthood can be defined as loving acts performed in the power of the Holy Spirit to meet the temporal and spiritual needs of those around us—and leaving the results to God.

The components of **biblical servanthood** involve:

1	Sacrifice.
2	Selflessness.
3	Loving someone despite the hurt they have or will cause you.

These acts aren't things you can physically see, but they're heart acts. Let's look at scriptures that delve deeper into sacrifice, selflessness and loving despite hurt. Remember, the results are left of to God. We aren't to look for equity in servanthood or preference. We're pleasing God when we walk as servants (prefer our spouse) in our marriage.

Number 1: Sacrifice

The ultimate display of **sacrifice** in marriage is found in Ephesians 5:25. It says Christ called the church his bride and gave His life for her. Jesus was willing to die and give up His life to save the church. He saw the end result and we were worth it to Him. The *New International Version* of Hebrews 12:2 says "...for the joy set before him he endured the cross, scorning its shame." Jesus, in his death made a mockery of the shame associated with crucifixion. The disciples couldn't conceptualize that He'd accept such an awful death when He had power to change the outcome. He did. However, the outcome He agreed to was greater than the pain and the shame. That's powerful!

This is how you can lay your "life" down. You want the end result, which is God healing you both wholly and completely, this too, is powerful!

As spouses, we're to be willing to sacrifice our lives for each other. Sacrifice means recognizing for the greater good of your marriage, family, and future generations; you release your viewpoint, stance, argument, and anger in exchange for God intervening. This is how you can lay your "life" down. You want the end result, which is God healing you <u>both</u> wholly and completely, this too, is powerful! As the article revealed, this can't be accomplished without the power of the Holy Spirit. You must leave the results up to God.

Number 2: Selflessness

The scripture for **selflessness** is in Ephesians 5:26 when Jesus said He was the groom, married to His bride (the church) and He washes her with the water of the Word. Another example of selflessness is when Jesus washed His disciple's feet before His betrayal and death. Washing someone's feet is also a symbol of love, preference, and humble servanthood.

In biblical days, it was the first act on entering the tent or house after a journey. Feet washing was refreshing as well as hygienic. In the case of ordinary people, the host furnished the water, and the guests washed their own feet, but in richer homes, the foot washing was done by a slave. It was viewed as the lowliest of all services. Jesus Himself modeled that **selflessness** is necessary and non-negotiable.

In John 13:5-17, Jesus told Peter you don't understand this now but one day you will, and as the Teacher, I must wash your feet. He also said, as a student, you'll do the same thing the Teacher does.

Luke 3:16 references John the Baptist stating he wasn't worthy to untie Jesus's sandals for cleaning. In biblical times, the person who cleaned sandals was also considered the least of the least. People walked and shared paths and roads with animals. When animals defecated on the road during travel, sometimes it was unavoidable and stepped in by those traveling; especially at night when lighting was low or null. To untie the laces of sandals and carry them was a menial task, carried out by a slave. Preferring your spouse over yourself requires selflessness. Willingly taking the role of a lowly slave can't be done without the power of the Holy Spirit. You must leave the results up to God. This is a truly powerful model! There's tremendous power in knowing you're a King yet humbling yourself as a servant.

> ### Preferring your spouse over yourself requires selflessness.

Number 3: Loving Continually

The scripture for **loving continually** despite hurt is Romans 5:5 and the *Good News Translation* says this hope does not disappoint us, for God has poured out his love into our hearts by means of the Holy Spirit, who is God's gift to us. We're never disappointed when we love our spouses despite hurt they've caused us because God promised He'd perfect it. Our role is to not give up hope.

Let me explain how your heart must continually remain healthy so that God's love can freely flow through it.

In the medical field, when a patient undergoes a heart bypass, it's because an artery has been clogged, blocked, or has plaque buildup that's causing diminished blood flow. *When blood isn't flowing at the proper rate and volume it'll cause major damage to the heart.* With this in mind, let's exchange the word blood with 'the love of God' and the word heart with 'marriage'.

It now reads:

> ## When the love of God isn't flowing at the proper rate and volume it'll cause major damage to the marriage.

So, what causes "plaque buildup" in your marriage? Well, the most common plaque builder is keeping a record of wrongdoing and not forgiving your spouse. This causes plaque buildup in your marriage and prevents love from flowing freely.

The *Contemporary English Bible* version of 1 Corinthians 13:5 says love isn't selfish or quick tempered. It doesn't keep a record of wrongs that others do.

The *New International Version* of John 13:7-17 displays how Jesus washed all His disciples' feet knowing that He would soon be betrayed. Jesus performed this selfless act while He was hurting, knowing that one of His own would betray Him. Again, He modeled for us that selfless love is possible even when your spouse hurts and betrays you. In spite of knowing that Judas would be the one to betray Him, He still washed his feet and took on the role of a lowly slave and fulfilled scripture. He told His disciples in verse 17 "you will do the same." Can I treat my spouse the same knowing he/she will betray me? It'll take power of the Holy Spirit, but it's possible. Jesus modeled it and we're not greater than our Teacher.

> ## Can I treat my spouse the same knowing he/she will betray me?

The *New Living Translation* of Hebrews 12:2 says, we do this by keeping our eyes on Jesus, the champion who initiates and perfects our faith. Because of the joy awaiting him, he endured the cross, disregarding its shame. Now He is seated in the place of honor beside God's throne.

I'll make this personal, *because of the joy awaiting Stacey, He endured the cross, disregarding its shame...* (Feel free to add <u>your</u> name).

I must ask the Lord to show me the joy awaiting Rozelle in his whole and complete state, just like Jesus did for me. That fuels me to endure through our pain and hardships. We've had our fair share of them but having a vision of my spouse whole and complete is a game-changer.

By faith, I speak life to him until what I'm shown is manifested in the natural. We, as married people are designed to become one to give honor to God and the covenant of marriage. It's the ultimate display of love and servanthood or humble preference between two people. I can't love Rozelle the way Jesus loves Him without the power of the Holy Spirit. It's impossible and I must leave the results up to God. Again, servanthood or preference involves sacrifice, selflessness, and loving someone despite the hurt they have or will cause you.

I put myself last and I'm serving the Lord when I prefer Rozelle. Rozelle puts himself last and is serving the Lord when he prefers me. As a servant of the Lord, I gladly prefer my husband because I should see him no different than Jesus himself. As human beings, this seems impossible but it's not. We tend to exhibit this manner of love often for our children who hurt us and cause us a lot of pain. We continue loving them despite the pain and strive to see the best in them.

I often ask myself, "Lord, if you're really Rozelle, how would I treat you?" Rozelle is my physical example of Jesus in that I'm honored to prefer him and be in his presence. Bear in mind, serving my spouse isn't to be confused with worshipping my spouse. In Lesson 22, I describe worship, and how dangerous it is to confuse it with preferring/serving with your spouse.

I must die to myself to see Rozelle as a representative of Jesus in our marriage. God is glorified when I serve him as I would Jesus Christ my

Lord and Savior as Ephesians 5:23 states. Rozelle does the same for me when he sees me a representative of Jesus in our marriage. Both parties have the same role of preferring each other and being willing servants.

Both parties have the same role of preferring each other and being willing servants.

You may ask, "How can I do this? I'm human with feelings, emotions, and live in a world where I'm programmed to think and act the opposite of this way." Simple. Model what Jesus showed us and transform your mind daily. It's a process that the Holy Spirit promised He'd assist us with. (Romans 12:1-2)

Jesus commanded us to love. He never requires from us what He hasn't already given Himself.

After all, Paul said in 2 Corinthians 4:17 that our light affliction is temporary yet carries a great eternal reward that far outweighs it. Affliction is also known as difficulty or hardship. Your transformational thinking process is your light affliction, and it has a great reward. Commit to it and push through to complete healing. The rejection, torture, bludgeoning, beating, and horrible death was Jesus's light affliction, and you and I are the eternal reward that far outweighed it.

The rejection, torture, bludgeoning, beating, and horrible death was Jesus's light affliction, and you and I are the eternal reward that far outweighed it.

So, what did Jesus do to prepare for His life of sacrificial love and a torturous death?

| 1 | He spent hours in prayer daily. |
| 2 | He fasted often. |

3	He crucified His flesh daily to remain connected to His servanthood role.

Therefore, He was prepared and able to endure the worst kind of physical death; being crucified.

I must spend time in prayer to remain connected to the Father and commit to fasting to crucify my fleshly body. Praying daily gives you directions and instructions on how to accomplish this in your marriage. Fasting is also not an option. I know I've inundated you with the importance of fasting in these lessons but, it's non-negotiable. If Jesus fasted then surely we're required to as well.

Marriage is spiritual and fasting is a spiritual concept that brings veritable results. (Matthew 6:17-18) Fasting kills your flesh and worldly way of thinking so you can grow spiritually. Live by the Spirit, don't be controlled by your fleshly body. The best plan to execute your earthly mission is to be a "dead man walking" so you can easily adopt the slave or servant role. It's very possible to put another human being's needs over yours. Jesus did it and He prayed for us while He was still on Earth, that we'd be able to do the same.

There's nothing I need that Rozelle can provide or fulfill without the help of the Holy Spirit. So why would I place that burden on a mere human? I don't.

The world teaches we are to be served and that our spouse is supposed to fulfill our needs. All lies. There's nothing I need that Rozelle can provide or fulfill without the help of the Holy Spirit. So why would I place that burden on a mere human? I don't. I worship his Creator, and in doing so, we're both provided for and fulfilled.

Can you imagine a world where married people viewed their spouse as a representative of the Lord Jesus and longed to please Him by preferring them selflessly, and left the results up to God? I'd venture to say there would be little, if any, strife, confusion, hatred, and divorce. That's the selfless love that Paul spoke about in Ephesians 5:25 when he said, Jesus laid down His life for His bride (the church). Your marriage is a part of the church. Your marriage was paid for by the blood of our Savior. Stop trying the secure the results that only God can provide, you'll continue to fall short.

Display **selfless love** and fight for your marriage. Create a marriage that your children and grandchildren are excited to emulate. The next generation is a part of your eternal reward as well. It begins and ends with **love and biblical servanthood,** which requires a lifestyle of prayer and fasting to remain humble before the Lord.

Let's pray:

Father, my daily goal is to please you with my words and actions. My actions are a direct reflection of what's in my heart. I understand the Holy Spirit's role is to search the hidden parts to reveal the areas that aren't pleasing to you. Lord, show me how to adopt the role of a humble servant and slave, as you modeled with your disciples, although you were the Teacher. Help me please you in my marriage by loving my spouse the way you've equipped me to. I'll please you Father by being **selfless, sacrificing and loving my spouse** despite the hurt they've caused me and may cause me in the future. When I center my thoughts on pleasing you, it has an eternal reward that far outweighs my sacrifice and pain. I know I must divest myself from how I've been taught and what the world teaches. Therefore, I'll pray and fast, and receive the support of the Holy Spirit in this ongoing, lifelong process. I want a marriage that my children and grandchildren are excited to emulate and give you the glory for its success. In Jesus's name, Amen.

Lesson 16

Married People Work
Through Divorce

The definition of divorce is two decrees.

The definition of division is two visions.

God's definition of marriage is one.

The *King James Bible* version of Genesis 2:24 says... and the two shall become one. Shall means over time or future tense. Prior to saying "I do" and during those early, difficult years, I wish I'd known that:

1	I'd experience (divorce) two decrees in my marriage, over and over, until we agreed on one.
2	I'd experience (division) two visions in my marriage, over and over, until we agreed about one vision.
3	This process is completely normal, and it didn't have to be as daunting as I experienced.

In other lessons, I've raised the point that the person you are today must be transformed into who God intended. The process of dying to yourself is not a one-time event, it's continual. This continual process has levels, and each level should produce more growth. Much like our schooling as children, each semester was designed with specific objectives and goals. The current semester presents knowledge that we must grasp, as it's cumulative and essential to our growth in the upcoming semester.

> **The process of dying to yourself is not a one-time event, it's continual.**

We're all a product of the sum of all our experiences and our childhood. All those experiences that don't align with the plan God has for you and your marriage, must be purged. When you reject or fight against a mandatory process it makes it even worse.

I will expound utilizing our financial management process.

Finances and money will be at the helm of many failed marriages because we have strong feelings and connections to finances as they represent among many things, our reward and survival.

I was raised in a household where my Mom was a better financial manager than my Dad and it was noticeably clear when my Dad was managing the household finances. I don't know who taught or didn't teach him about financial management, but we all writhed when he managed the money. He was the primary source of income when we were younger, and my Mom was a "domestic engineer," as she fondly called herself. Today, they're referred to as stay-at-home-Moms.

During their early years of marriage, some of their biggest arguments were about money and how bills should be paid. It was a point of contention and you could feel the passion when it was being discussed. As a child, I understood that bills should be paid on time and you should live within your means. I also learned that your creditors are human beings, who want to be communicated with when you can't pay them as agreed.

My Mom was of the school that "we pay our bills first and we'll eat with what's left." My husband had the opposite school of thought based on how he watched his Mom manage their finances. He said, she believed in "eating good first and paying bills with the remainder."

Coming from opposite backgrounds caused major crisis for us in this area. After being married for a few months, we met to discuss our finances and debt. That meeting emerged as the biggest argument we'd had to date and ended with him throwing the bill file folder across the room. I remember saying to myself, "Oh my God, I married Terry Prater (my Dad), and this is going to be hell on Earth."

Having two decrees in this area meant learning to work together and settling on one decree. We didn't know how to work together and how entrenched we were in our own experiences. Not to mention, being resolute that we (individually) were NOT going to change, and the issue was with the other person.

I didn't realize how finances evoked fear and disappointment in me from my childhood, and how much pain I associated with a lack of money. I witnessed and deduced that a lack of available money is completely different from lack, due to poor money management. Ours was completely the latter. Rozelle and I always made a good living, and we were blessed to have enjoyed professional careers and owned businesses.

In the earlier years of our marriage, we adopted the "roommate" plan where we split everything down the middle to avoid conflict and this worked for a while. We later adopted a one year on/off program where one of us would solely manage the finances for a year, while the other contributed blindly. The one solely managing, instituted their own rules and when it was time to exchange hands it caused so much confusion. You were tasked with undoing the current structure and restructuring it to fit the next person's managing style. It was a disaster. We refused to submit to one decree because we were unwavering that our individual plan was best. Although wildly dysfunctional, it worked because we both agreed on it. We didn't realize that settling for temporary, make-shift agreements, to avoid conceding our pride would make our poor financial matters worse over time.

> **We didn't realize that settling for temporary, make-shift agreements, to avoid conceding our pride would make our poor financial matters worse over time.**

Rozelle, at one point, carried so much pain in his heart towards me before his breakthrough (see Lesson 2) that he'd penalize me by not letting me interject in the finances. I knew this was his approach, so I'd make it truly clear that I was better at managing than him. This back and forth went on and on for years. I finally got tired of the conflict and conceded. It wasn't what I wanted, but at the time, it was the best way to manage my stress so I could focus on other, more important things.

We walked around our mountain of pride and deception for decades. Our two-decree financial management plan yielded nothing of lasting value. We eventually had to file bankrupt and saw our credit scores plummet from the high 790's to below 600. We learned through hardship, that maintaining two decrees had prolonged, damaging effects which weren't worth it, because the work we underwent to repair our messes was counter-productive and more stressful. After 15 years of counter-productive decrees, steeped in pride and fear, we were finally primed and ready to submit to God's will for us in this area.

The Parable of the Sower in Matthew 13 speaks of reaping a thirtyfold, sixtyfold, or hundredfold harvest from sowing. After we submitted to God's will and relinquished our pride, over time, we slowly crept from thirtyfold, then to sixtyfold in our finances. We rebuilt our credit, savings and investments and we were very comfortable financially. However, there was still more work to face and achieve to reach hundredfold.

Years later, in prayer I began receiving direction from the Lord to begin large scale projects that I knew would require an overhaul of our current structure, and that required surrendering to God individually first.

The Lord showed us there were still remnants of rejection, abandonment, pride, fear, and trust entangled with our financial management roots and that was prohibiting us from hundredfold. We needed an improvement to complete the projects that were on the table, and the Lord orchestrated the perfect setting for it.

Prior to this revelation, I was working in CA, and one morning in prayer the Lord instructed me to start working more closely with Rozelle on our finances. I was immediately stricken with fear and grief. I said, "Lord please tell me why we need to revisit this topic again? Let's just leave it the way it is. It's working absolutely fine. Besides, you remember how much of a fool he acts if things aren't exactly his way." He'd been solely managing the finances for the past six years or so with my limited input. I knew he had strong feelings about them, and I was too consumed in so many other obligations to be more integrally involved.

By this time in our marriage, we'd grown in our personal relationships with the Lord and learned how to go to Him about ourselves, instead of venting about the other person. God always works on us as individuals before He can connect us as a couple. Always.

God always works on us as individuals before He can connect us as a couple. Always.

Over the next few months, I completely ignored the Lord's instructions. Sure enough, we entered a season where there were major transitions that required us to know the exact status of our income streams. I worked in healthcare as a consultant and had been extremely fortunate to retain consistent contracts for years. After I didn't take heed to the instructions the Lord gave me, a few months later, I was without a contract/income for the first time in over ten years. It was a disaster. I was depressed and thought, "Wait. Why are we here AGAIN?" However, I had no need to complain because I knew the answer, I ignored the warning, and it wasn't worth it!

Now, we had to scramble and restructure everything to meet our monthly financial obligations. Had I listened and followed His instructions when I received them, we would've been more prepared and breezed through that season. Through this process, I learned that it was no longer good for us to continue our current structure just as the Lord stated.

In addition to the word of warning in CA, a few months prior to that I was praying and asking for more agreement in our marriage and for us to be closer. I also prayed for the Lord to continue to heal our past pain. I couldn't fathom that He'd use our finances to bridge the gap in all three of these areas. He healed us by eradicating some root systems below ground, that manifested itself above ground, as disagreement in financial management.

We had to be honest and face our underlying fears. I chose to not be involved in our finances because everything I tried over the years didn't work and caused more defeat. I was fearful of repeating my early childhood days of feeling there was never enough. I didn't like the stress it caused so I avoided it. Rozelle was fearful of being rejected and abandoned and only trusted himself to provide. He felt if he weren't intricately involved somehow he'd be left out. We fought each other rather than allowing the Lord to address our underlying issues. This season uprooted those fears and we conquered them.

We, as Christians, are supposed to rely on the Lord for our provision. Provision means "for the vision," and when we pray for the Lord to bless our finances, essentially we're praying that we align ourselves to His vision, not our own. Once we align ourselves and submit to His perfect plan, He'll release the "for" (pro) to accomplish **His** vision.

Following this 16-month process, we started divesting from how society views finance and defines financial success. We organized our incomes based on the vision God specifically gave us. We witnessed expedient healing from our past issues and our financial harvest was speedily too!

I must clarify that being a good steward over and effectively managing your finances is the <u>only</u> prerequisite to receive more. This wasn't an overnight process. We set out to manage our money together with one vision, one decree and one goal in mind, and that's when the explosive growth happened for us. Had we not involved the Lord I'm sure we'd still be receiving sixtyfold harvests. As I reference in Lesson 2, we committed to weekly meetings, in-depth discussions, and then we put new processes in place.

> **We set out to manage our money together with one vision, one decree and one goal in mind, and that's when the explosive growth happened for us.**

I didn't realize how stubborn I was until I was faced with this trial. It took a full year of weekly meetings and mature communication to form an iron-clad system. A system that both of us understood and agreed on. We made the decision that we wouldn't focus on the time it took to repair the damage; we were committed to the process. The fighting stopped and the communication started. The forgiveness flowed freely rather than the accusations. We walked in humility and patience toward each other as the Father directs us to and now we're finally married (adopted one decree) in this area!

I'm grateful for our process because it made our healing and testimony that much more impactful.

Our lessons learned are:

1	To seek the Lord as individuals about our own issues and He started healing us individually.
2	To stop looking at each other as the enemy but as an ally.
3	To recognize how much, we individually received grace and mercy to get past our pain and childhood issues.
4	To give that same grace and mercy to each other.
5	To remain (married) one in this area.

The forgiveness flowed freely rather than the accusations.

Per my opening statement, Genesis 2:24 says...and the two shall become one. Shall denotes a process over time. I chose our finances to elaborate on having two decrees and how the Lord's plan for us answered multiple petitions I placed before Him. It truly pays to trust in the Lord as He does all things perfectly and in seamless timing.

Now, I want you to honestly look closely at ANY area of your marriage where there are two decrees operating at the same time. Regardless to how they seem to be functioning well presently, you **know** in your heart that it's not God's vision for your marriage. You know that you aren't receiving hundredfold returns so take it to the Lord in prayer. I want you to experience the sheer joy of seeing unabridged life in this area of your marriage.

Having two decrees prohibits growth and it's a breeding ground for stagnation and decreased potential. Please don't ignore or try to reason your way out of whatever the Lord instructs you to do, trust me, it's not worth it. The Lord blesses agreement. It begins with you asking the Lord to heal **you** first. Your spouse shouldn't be the focus of your prayers in whatever area you're believing for. There's always individual work that must be done <u>before</u> the Lord connects the two of you together. Start working on yourself and I guarantee God's plan is going to yield hundredfold harvests. You can't even fathom the peace and explosive growth that's in store for you!

Living abundantly is peaceful, gratifying and included in the vision God has for you and it has innumerable rewards.

Let's pray:

Lord, please forgive me for leaning on my own limited understanding, concerning finances and how they should be managed in my marriage/household. While I live on Earth money is our currency and necessary for survival, however, whatever I'm holding on to from my past that's causing disruption and lack, please reveal it. I need you to create an opportunity for healing to occur. Your orchestrated opportunities are always perfect. Holy Spirit give me the strength to face what's belowground and eradicate it forever. I know your will includes continuous growth, season after season, and I/we need your help. Show us how to save, invest, and be excellent stewards over what you've placed in our hands financially. Lead us to the proper person(s), books, seminars, and subject matter experts to enhance our knowledge. Lord, just as you gave Abraham a customized plan to follow for his life, we yield ourselves to hear our customized plan today. My spouse and I won't operate under two decrees because it embezzles from what you created for us as ONE. I thank you in advance for complete health and healing in my marriage. I thank you for testimonies that'll bless other couples and glorify your name. In Jesus's name, Amen.

Lesson 15

Beautiful Scars

*T*here's a beautiful song by Matthew West titled, *The Healing Has Begun* (2010) and one of my favorite lyrics says, "So don't be afraid to show them your beautiful scars, cause they're the proof..."

This song resonated with me so intensely during a season in 2015 when I was being prepared for public ministry. The Lord started working on my heart first. After at least nine months of speaking and praying death over my life, death showed up.

Between the years of 2011 through 2014, I had so many major life events and changes that took place, I felt totally exhausted and out of control.

In every area, there were challenges: health, family, finances, and my career.

In my health, I was experiencing perimenopause and the first one of my six sisters to do so. I also lost my Dad during this time and we moved back home to Michigan, after living south for 13 years. Moving back to Michigan during a depressed economy necessitated taking a

60% pay cut to remain in my career field. I also shifted from consulting to full time work while facing my first-born's college tuition expenses. It was an extremely trying time to say the least.

This season began what I like to call my "new life after death."

Life, at times, deals you a hand that you must play, whether you're willing or not. This season began what I like to call my "new life after death." So why did I pray for death? Well, life didn't seem to be worth living at that time. I knew God was incredible and I'd seen His hand time and time again, but I felt like, "I'm just tired of the race and I want off of the track!"

I'd given up mentally and it was just a matter of time that my body would align with my thoughts. It did. My hormones were going haywire, and I learned during one of our couples' therapy sessions that I was "too unhealthy to make sound decisions." Our therapist suspected that I had a chemical imbalance and would benefit from being treated by someone who specialized in clinical therapy. That was one of the lowest days of my life. Soon after, I was diagnosed with generalized anxiety disorder and chemical depression and placed on several medications.

Just when I thought things couldn't get any worse, they did. Tyler Perry's movie *Madea's Big Happy Family* (2011) has a scene, where Madea explains how your forties is the most stressful decade. She said you're dealing with teenagers, transitions, body/health changes, aging parents, mid-life crisis and everything else all **at the same time**. No truer words have been spoken. Most days, I had just enough energy to go to work, return home, and get back in bed. My diet of choice was ice cream and red wine. I lived in one room of my then, 4500 square foot home, away from my husband and children. I only spent time with friends who wanted to hang out and have fun as I was depleted of the ability to face pain or deal with any problems. Little did I know then that death was coming, but the resurrection afterwards changed the course of my life forever!

Little did I know then that death was coming, but the resurrection afterwards changed the course of my life forever!

It was February 15, 2015 and I was working as a consultant in Providence, RI. It was one of the coldest winters this area had seen in 100 years. That month over 60 inches of snow fell in the Northeast. It was brutal, even for me, a mid-westerner who'd just coped with Michigan's polar vortex winter the year prior.

I was teaching software to physicians and clinical staff and parking spaces at the training facility were minimal. They designated off-site parking lots for the consultants to park that required a shuttle to bring us to the buildings. If you were lucky and got to work early enough, you could land a spot relatively close enough to walk without waiting for the shuttle in the sub-below temps. I created a strategy to minimize feeling the cold. I'd get to the training facility, sit in my car with the heat blasting on high for at least ten minutes to warm up. By the time I got out of my car, and made a mad dash across the parking lot, I wouldn't feel the bone chilling wind around me. That was my routine every morning upon arriving to work.

One night, I had a lucid dream that I was backing into one of the parking spaces at the facility when suddenly, my car didn't stop although I was hitting the brake. I remember seeing one of my co-workers sitting in her car and we made eye contact.

I knew the car was going to bump the car next to it if I didn't hit the brakes but again, it wouldn't stop. Within seconds, I felt what was my spirit springing off my shoulders as if it were using my body as a platform to jump in the air. A moment later I heard a loud "clump," that sounded just like the noise you hear when the power suddenly goes out. Immediately, I felt my body fall against the steering wheel and that was it. I died. Seconds later I was in total darkness. Darkness so thick you could cut it. Although I was dead, I could hear and feel every emotion. I heard the EMT workers conversing with Rozelle about how I died in the car and my coworker saw me and called for help.

I began to scream so loud and so long, I'd have to stop and take in more air. I screamed repeatedly, "JESUS, HELP ME!" I was thinking, "Why am I in darkness? Wait, I'm not supposed to be **here**!" As fast as I could think a thought, the answer returned to me seconds later in my thoughts.

I heard people speaking well of me at my funeral, but I wasn't in heaven and at peace.

The Holy Spirit would say, "Stacey, you prayed for death." Then, I would scream louder and louder, "NO, NO, NO, NO! Jesus, help me!" This process of hearing what was going on in the physical world but experiencing death and darkness went on for what felt like hours. I heard people speaking well of me at my funeral, but I wasn't in heaven and at peace.

The Holy Spirit would quietly say, "Stacey, you didn't do what you were supposed to do. You didn't finish your work." I'd continue screaming and I remember thinking, "Wait, I've heard preachers and pastors say if you get tired of running this race, you can pray and ask God to take you home." The Holy Spirit gently whispered, "That's not in my Word." I was going insane and there was no relief at all! It was torturing to have a thought, and then the answer come as fast as the thought finishes. The torment of being fully alive in your thoughts, but consumed in complete darkness, was debilitating and horrific to say the least. I kept wailing "The blood of Jesus, the blood of Jesus!" over and over, to the point of gasping and collapse.

Suddenly, I was back in my bedroom looking down at my dead body. I screamed "The blood of Jesus" again and at that exact moment, I was back in my body and sat straight up. Soaking in sweat, I jumped out of bed and ran and sat in my recliner to catch my breath. I was physically exhausted. I was so afraid yet relieved that it was just a lucid dream, but I know **beyond the shadow of a doubt,** that it was REAL. It was more than real. I felt every emotion and it scared me so much that I was shaking uncontrollably. I sat in my recliner and cried so much my eyes were nearly swollen shut. I muttered through my tears, "Lord, please help me, I don't want to die and not see your face in peace."

I heard the Lord say, "Go to your email inbox and search for that video Rozelle sent to you on December 31, 2011; you saved it." I found and watched a YouTube video about the church and how the placebo drug that some Christians "take" is thinking we're saved, in right standing, but not fulfilling our work which causes overwhelming discontentment. It also discussed being lulled to sleep by media and the way the world believes.

I'm confident that everyone will one day know who Jesus is, and be held responsible for their time spent on Earth. Every single person.

Included in the video was a detailed testimony of a pastor who suffered exactly what I had in my earth-shattering lucid dream. I was relieved yet traumatized to know that I experienced death and the most horrendous part was my soul was very much alive! I was alive, but forever lost and separated from the Lord. I'm confident that everyone will one day know who Jesus is, and be held responsible for their time spent on Earth. Every single person.

I also learned from the video that the Lord's love for me allowed me to go through that lucid death dream. From that moment forth, I didn't need anyone to ever tell me Jesus is real! I know He is. There's also work that must be completed for those who answer the call and give their lives to Him. My specific purpose for being on Earth needed to be discovered and fulfilled. That event marked the resurrection of Stacey Lyn Prater-White. My new journey began, and my life was forever changed for the better. I began to diligently seek the Lord for myself. I researched and found that seek means to give maximum effort.

I gave my entire life over to God and day by day, I began to see small changes. After a few months, noticeable changes were seen by others. It wasn't easy to fight my former way of thinking and behaviors, but I was committed to the process, and God's abundant grace was available to me daily.

The difference in my life as a Christian prior to this dream was, I hadn't said yes to **my purpose and life's work.** My custom life's work is mandatory and non-negotiable. Afterwards, I re-committed my relationship with the Lord and asked the Holy Spirit to show me step by step what to do.

He said, "We had to begin at the beginning." Before receiving new seeds for planting, you must clear all the weeds and everything unhealthy that's in the soil. For me, the soil was my heart. I began to have dreams about being a child about six years old. These series of dreams would display periods of my life on a motion picture screen, and I'd narrate what was happening.

One scene showed me getting a spanking from my Dad for not going to bed on time and playing with my siblings, although I didn't deserve it. This night, I hid under the bed and went to sleep because I knew we'd all get in trouble if he had to come in our room for playing around instead of going to sleep. More often than not, my parents would send us to bed, and we'd keep laughing, frolicking, and making noise well past our bedtime.

Like clockwork, my Dad would come in our rooms with his belt, and everyone would get a spanking. This night one of my sisters said, "Daddy, Stacey is hiding under the bed." He called my name a few times and I didn't answer. He called again forcefully, and I said "Daddy, I'm sleep."

He then lifted the bed up with one arm and dragged me out from under it with his other hand. He gave me a spanking, but I remember making eye contact with him, and staring at him for about five seconds. He knew that I knew, he gave me a spanking just to save face in front of the rest of the children, not because I was one of the ones playing and really deserved it.

The Holy Spirit said, "That's where the root of bitterness began in you. You didn't like that your parents believed in corporate punishments to manage such a big family. You also felt like their religious beliefs was the reason for having so many children." As a child my thought was, if there were less children, then they could manage them and know exactly who was guilty or innocent instead of punishing the entire group.

I greatly resented this style of punishment and it festered and appeared in my actions towards my siblings. I also felt bitter about the religious rules that were taught in the former churches we attended as children that weren't biblically sound. I knew as a child that something wasn't quite right, but I didn't know how to verbalize it.

I cried while looking at myself on this screen and ask the Lord to help me release my anger and bitterness. I knew the roots were effecting my current life and how I processed anger and closed myself off emotionally at times.

From that moment forward the compilation of pain and resentment I carried for over 40 years was gone.

At the end of this motion picture dream, the Lord said, "Now that we've reasoned together Stacey, I'll wash you white as snow." From that moment forward the compilation of pain and resentment I carried for over 40 years was gone.

The scripture reference for "come let us reason together" is found in Isaiah 1:18-19, God was tired of the sins Judah committed while they were in Jerusalem and explained how they totally lost sight of His commands and statutes. He asked them to reason together. That would be the equivalent of being in a court case and all the evidence is presented. The Lord wants you to confess what you've done and why you've done it. However, unlike an earthly human judge, He knows the **root** of why you conduct yourself the way you do. Instead of sentencing you to punishment, He heals you and makes you whole because of His love for you. He'll reveal to you where your thoughts began to take root and the corresponding actions from those thoughts.

I never would've imagined that the root system to my anger stemmed from six years old. Only the Holy Spirit can search the hidden chambers of our hearts. (Jeremiah 17: 9-10) Ironically, when I asked the clinical therapist at approximately what age, did she suspect my chemical imbalance began, she said age six. I was floored. God showed me how repressed anger was still wreaking havoc in my life at that present time.

When I researched Psalm 51:7, I found that "wash you white as snow" was a reverse process from dyeing garments in ancient times. To take a white garment and dye it to the color of scarlet was a tedious double-dye process. Scarlet was a fast or fixed color. Neither dew, nor rain, washing, or long usage, would remove it. Once the dyeing process was complete, it was thought to be **impossible** for the garment to return to the beginning bright white color. God said only He could because He created all of the knowledge, rudiments, supplies, and processes for double-dyeing, and nothing is hidden from Him.

Day by day and step by step, He reversed the pain and shame I carried from my sins by washing me. He replaced my anger with joy and a zeal for life! It was a euphoric feeling knowing I was "under construction" and once finished, I'd **never** have to endure those pains again. I experienced dreams like this night after night for months. They all resulted in healing my heart of various issues, pain and trauma, and new seeds of joy being planted.

One night, it was different. I was in a surgery suite and I was laying on the operating table with all my street clothes on and clinging to my purse. The Holy Spirit was pleading with me to get prepared for the surgery I consented to, but I was terrified. He said, "Stacey, you must get ready because Jesus is coming to start your case and if you're not prepped and ready, He will leave, then you'll miss your opportunity." Jesus came to my surgery suite and saw the Holy Spirit pleading with me and He said, "Once I'm done with the other cases, I'll check back in here, but if she's not undressed and prepped, I will leave."

Working in the medical field over the years, I've assisted doctors with their patient's medical records and witnessed patients miss their scheduled surgery time slot because the pre-op checklist wasn't complete. Sometimes, if the outstanding items were minor, the surgeon would shift the schedule and circle back around to their case.

Jesus said, "Stacey, you must wear this. No one will know the work I've done if they don't see your scars. I have scars too."

With that example in mind, I knew time was of the essence. Reluctantly, I consented and got prepped. In the next scene, I was on the surgery table and Jesus was repairing parts inside my body. When He was finished, He brought this horrible looking blanket that had scars all over it to cover me with. I screamed, "No Lord! I don't want that on me, it's ugly and has keloids and scars all over it!" Jesus sweetly said, "Stacey you must wear this. No one will know the work I've done if they don't see your scars. I have scars too." I saw the tears running down my face as He wrapped me in this scarred blanket.

I woke up from that dream and I was different. I could feel it. I had a boldness and confidence I've never had before. Miraculously, I was totally comfortable with my scars and I understood, in reality, they were my personal testimonies of God's love and goodness in my life. It was nothing to be ashamed of, but to be celebrated.

Later that morning, I had coffee with my sister and shared my encounter. I told her I could hear myself speaking to people in that dream and sharing all of my "scars", and how God turned them into "stars" for His glory.

Soon after that dream, I called my daughter who was away in college and having some difficulties. I told her about my full college experience from beginning to end. I shared my insecurities, immense pain from my Mom's sudden death, breaking off my engagement to Rozelle, unwanted pregnancy, and how I spun completely out of control. My erratic behavior resulted in me losing my academic scholarship. She needed to hear the word of my testimony and how I overcame all of those scars by the blood of the Lamb (Revelation 12:11). I was free from pride and embarrassment. I was free after that "surgery" to begin giving hope through my testimony of survival. Jesus kept me and saved me, and I wanted to see others free as well.

Within a few months, I was led to start hosting bible studies in my home. Each month, my sister Clarissa and I would cook and invite women over to share the Word of God. It was wonderful, and each month my confidence grew more and more. I realized it was needful to have small, intimate gatherings where women could study the Word, encourage each other, and pray. I began walking in my God-given purpose and didn't give up when things didn't go as planned. I knew the rewards would come from diligence.

Synchronously, life was still processing me every day like everyone else and I wasn't exempt from pain and hardship. I was still learning and growing as a sister, wife, mother, aunt, and friend. Some days I felt totally inept, but I know feelings change. I had setbacks and some losses, but never have I felt defeated since that lucid dream. I study the Word of God and it sustains me when I'm low and lose steam. The *New Living Translation* of Psalm 119:11 says, "I have hidden your word in my heart that I might not sin against you." I like one of the cross-referenced scriptures in Psalm 4:4 that says, don't sin by letting anger control you. Think about it overnight and remain silent.

He uprooted the anger that was controlling me and planted seeds of love and patience.

That resonated with me because overnight is referring to sleeping and being quiet. Jesus talks to me when I'm sleeping and through dreams. He uprooted the anger that was controlling me and planted seeds of love and patience. They continue to grow to this day.

Ask the Lord to search your heart before you go to sleep and be sure to ask for forgiveness if you're holding onto anger. When you wake up, be obedient to the instructions He gives you. They'll have an everlasting impact.

I don't believe that I would've been equipped to share His Word in this capacity had I not hit rock bottom. The *King James Bible* version of Hebrews 11:6 says, He that comes to God must first believe that He is and that He rewards those who diligently seek Him. I believed that God existed prior to my death experience, but I didn't diligently seek Him. I came to Him begging for death and questioning my reasons for being here on Earth.

He answered me in that dream and the rewards have been indescribable since!

Above all, each, and everything you've encountered up to this very moment He'll use to bring glory to Himself.

Diligence is careful and persistent work. As I've detailed throughout these lessons, I challenge you to go hard after God, carefully and persistently and I guarantee, He'll blow your mind! Above all, each, and everything you've encountered up to this very moment He'll use to bring glory to Himself.

So, don't be afraid to show off those beautiful scars, they're proof that He loves you beyond your human comprehension and died to save you from eternal darkness.

Let's pray:

Father, please give me another opportunity to reason with you. I know you'll wash me and make me whole. Your love has covered my sins and I have a distinct purpose for being here. I won't give up. I know my best life is one quality decision away. You sent me a helper in the person of the Holy Spirit who understands exactly what I'm going through, and He has complete solutions. Holy Spirit give me courage to say yes wholeheartedly. I won't allow pride and embarrassment to keep me from all that you've meticulously created just for ME. I'll put maximum effort into learning about you and your plan for me. I'll completely lean on and trust you through this process. Thank you for removing every pain that I carry that'll result in beautiful scars. In Jesus's name, Amen.

4-Pillar Marriage

*I*n 2017, I was fortunate to lead a group of wonderful young women through a nine-month mentoring program. I was also blessed to work with a team of leaders who are formidable forces by their own right. A few months prior to the birth of this program, I'd been consulting the Lord about what He wanted me to do in the upcoming season. I'd begun hosting monthly Bible studies in my home a year prior and they were fun and impactful. I didn't know if I was to continue going in this direction, so I inquired and one morning and while preparing my classroom for physician training, I kept seeing a table with four legs. Finally, I asked the Lord, "What does that mean?" At the same time, I could clearly hear the scripture "If I be lifted up, I'll draw all men unto me." (John 12:32)

I said, "Lord but what does that have to do with this table?" He said, "Those legs are pillars, and the top of the table is the platform I use to build your purpose on." I said, "Okay, well what do those four pillars represent?"

He explained:

1	Your spiritual life.
2	Your health (mentally and physically).
3	Your family/relationships.
4	Your career/finances.

I was intrigued and sat quiet for a few minutes to ponder this. Then I asked," What does 'be lifted up' truly mean?"

After work, I searched the scripture in John 12:32 to better understand the context and who the audience was at the time. Jesus was speaking to his disciples and explaining to them the type of death He'd endure. From His death and resurrection life would come for all who believed. Jesus being lifted up also represented His ascension to Heaven.

When speaking with His disciples, He also referenced Moses lifting up the serpent on the pole in the Old Testament (Numbers 21:8-9). In the wilderness, when the Children of Israel were sick and dying from the serpent's venomous bite, those who looked up at it on the pole were healed. The very thing that caused them sickness and death was used to bring healing and life.

In addition to these scriptures, I also studied fatal snake bites, venom, anti-venom, and how these things were connected to Jesus being lifted. According to Wikipedia, *antivenom is made by collecting venom from the relevant animal and injecting small amounts of it into a domestic animal. The antibodies that form is then collected from the domestic animal's blood and purified.*

The Holy Spirit showed me that Jesus's blood is **our** antivenom and no matter how sick, diseased, or deadly our "pillars" are; He is the only solution to life! Often times were convinced that certain areas of our lives are far too complex and appear irreparable. We settle and give up and that's not what His death and resurrection accomplished. Again, His death and resurrection brought life and solutions.

> ### The Holy Spirit showed me that Jesus's blood is our antivenom and no matter how sick, diseased, or deadly our "pillars" are; He is the only solution to life!

> Complementing the World Health Organization's definition, *antivenoms work by boosting our immune response after a snakebite. They are made by immunizing donor animals such as horses or sheep with snake venoms. These animals have robust immune systems and produce powerful antibodies that can bind to snake venom components, enabling our own immune defenses to eliminate these toxins. Antivenoms are obtained by harvesting and then purifying the antibodies from plasma produced by the donor animal.* **Good quality antivenoms can literally make a difference between life and death.**

After studying antivenom and comparing it to the biblical references, I concluded, Jesus's blood also has the only powerful antibodies that can bind to any venom component, enabling us to eliminate toxins. His blood redeemed us and purified us from ANY sickness including **how we think**.

Jesus is the only real quality "antivenom" that makes a difference between life and death.

I was excited to link these scriptures illustrating that Jesus is the answer for all areas of healing, and the firm foundation we stand upon. Regardless to the instability of your pillars, Jesus is the One who can build and strengthen them causing others to want to receive Him. Therefore, He draws all men unto Him.

I started asking the Holy Spirit about my table pillars and which ones needed work. He said, "Draw an honest depiction of your table based on your maturity and stability in these areas."

He said, "Draw an honest depiction of your table based on your maturity and stability in these areas."

I sat and physically sketched a picture of what my table would look like and the legs/pillars weren't even at all. None of them were even close in height. Then, I imagined what the platform would look like atop of those uneven pillars/legs. Essentially, it wouldn't be useful, as it was very unstable.

Next, I recalled the countless times I was annoyed while sitting or eating at a table and the legs weren't even. It's the worse. I also thought about how you really can't utilize a table that has one unstable leg because it can't handle its true weight capacity. It'll eventually fall because it's not balanced. If it's true of tables, it's true of our lives, if one leg/pillar is unstable, no matter which one it is, when weight is applied, it'll eventually fall.

All these scenarios and images kept repeatedly surfacing in my mind. I sat and stared at my sketch and my career/finances pillar was the tallest one. I'd invested 30+ years into my career and it was very fruitful. It didn't compare to the height of the other 3 pillars. I knew I had work to do. The Lord told me, "Let's work on making those other pillars as tall and strong as your career/finance one."

Naturally, I thought the primary direction would be aimed toward my spiritual life. It wasn't. It was **all four** pillars being strengthened at the same time. I knew I'd have to lean on the Holy Spirit for direction because I wasn't clear on what to do or where to start.

The *Berean Study Bible* version of Proverbs 3:6 says, in **all** your ways acknowledge Him, and He will make your paths straight. I carefully studied that scripture and found that acknowledging Him means consulting the Lord about the things you already know how to do.

For example, I don't use my GPS to drive to work because I'm very familiar with the route. However, I may not know about an accident, road construction or a stalled vehicle on any particular day. So, when I watch the news or listen to the radio for traffic updates while getting ready for work, I'm essentially acknowledging those who are watching the traffic closely, and then I determine the best route to take that day. Therefore, humility is acknowledging the Lord about what you know how to do but deferring to His plan, because He knows from day to day what lies ahead of us.

I was led to research one of my favorite scriptures, 3 John 1:2. Let's look at these three different translations:

Dear friend, I pray that you may prosper in every way and be in good health physically just as you are spiritually. (Holman Christian Standard)	**Dear friend, I hope all is well with you and that you are as healthy in body as you are strong in spirit.** (New International Version)	**Beloved, I wish above all things that thou mayest prosper and be in health, even as thy soul prospereth.** (King James Version)

As I studied this scripture in different translations, I understood the focus was to be intentional about all areas of your life, knowing that your **soul** is the pacesetter. I asked myself was my soul prospering like my career was. No, not at all.

> **I asked myself, was my soul prospering like my career was. No, not at all.**

According to the scripture, my health, family, relationships, career, and finances follow the pace at which my **soul** sets. I needed to shift my attention because my soul will live forever, long after I leave this Earth. When your soul is your first priority, the other areas will align and leave a legacy on Earth as well. It can't be the other way around. All these pillars should testify of the goodness of God in your life.

Here's another example, I was at my son's United States Air Force BMT Graduation, and proud to learn that he was selected as an Honors graduate. He was in the top ten percent of his 800 person Airmen class. During the ceremony, when they were marching and a line of men passed by, at one point, the line of four men looked like **one** person was marching. They were all functioning in lockstep as one unit. It was amazing. I know that level of precision took a lot of practice to achieve. The Lord spoke to me and said, "That's what it looks like when all four pillars are prospering, no one is ahead of the next; it's one strong unit."

I was led to start a fast shortly after having this conversation and this is where I received so much more revelation about myself. I also discovered how to properly build and strengthen my pillars simultaneously. In this season, I was given a strict schedule to follow that didn't allow for much social time.

For my **spiritual pillar**, I spent most of my free time listening to and watching videos that focused on our ministry's mission. We believe marriage and family is the space God wants us to explicate. I watched countless videos of Dr. Myles Munroe and read his books on prayer, men, women, and leadership. I established a lifestyle of prayer and fasting that included a component of continual service. I allotted time in my schedule to meet and minister to women and share the Word of God.

At the same time, the Lord started showing me some of the areas in my heart that weren't pleasing to Him and how to work through them. It was difficult at times and of course, I cried a lot in this season. I stored a lot of anger in my heart for things I couldn't control. I was angry and bitter about so many things that I detailed in Lessons 15 and 23. Essentially, the Lord couldn't plant new seeds until He uprooted the things that were contaminated and venomous. I was surprised to learn I had dysfunctional adult behaviors that stemmed from my childhood as early as six years old.

Isaiah 58:6-14 speaks of the fast the Lord approves and what the intended outcome will be. He details several if-then scenarios which proves that fasting can be done improperly and yield nothing of value. However, when done correctly as he outlined, fasting will produce great benefits.

Fasting is 100 percent inward and personal. Fasting changes you, not other people.

Fasting is 100 percent inward and personal. Fasting changes you, not other people. The outcome of my fasts highlighted how negative my thinking was and how I lived in constant fear.

I was tasked with creating confessions ladened with the Word of God to correct years of hurting behaviors. I wrote them out, typed them up, displayed them around my home and even emailed them to myself. In some cases, I created voice notes in my phone and had Siri read them to me if I was driving. When a negative thought would surface, I'd immediately attack it using God's word and my confessions. In the beginning, it didn't seem as if it was helping, but I didn't stop. The Holy Spirit would assure me it was at work and taking root, and I had to be patient. Immediately I began sleeping so much better and didn't have anxiety attacks as much. Over time, my anxiety attacks totally went away.

I was growing in the Lord and able to observe why the smallest of things prohibited my peace. They, in fact, weren't small things to the Lord. The Lord showed me I had a list of people I'd offended. I called, texted, met for coffee, emailed, or physically visited them so I could apologize. A few of the people He showed me, I was unaware I'd even hurt with my actions. Fasting will reveal things you may have forgotten, but the Lord will uncover them so you can face and correct them. Fasting is powerful!

Clearly, these changes overflowed into my marriage and family. Slowly and methodically, I started seeing changes for the better in my relationship with Rozelle and our children. The biggest change I noticed was my patience. I spoke life about them more and protected the peace in our home. It was a process, don't get me wrong, but I didn't allow fussing and bickering with the children to fester. I knew I had to model the behavior I wanted to manifest, so Rozelle and I confronted the challenge of talking things out and not arguing about petty things.

We also instituted an hour of prayer on Sunday mornings and Wednesday evenings and only Christian music was to be played in the mornings while the children were getting ready for school. Although I was focusing on myself and my spiritual pillar was being strengthened, my family benefited from my decision to be diligent.

My **health pillar** was incorporated in a unique fashion. The Lord started highlighting how emotional I was. My fear and emotions went hand in hand. He directed me to change my diet first. I ate a lot of sweets and carbs. I also noticed when I'd drink coffee my emotions would be heightened. At my age, I wasn't producing the same ratio of hormones that I needed to be balanced, so I had to ensure I was eating the right foods that supplemented them. The Lord gave me a lifestyle diet to follow that was perfect for me.

Once again, this was a difficult transition because I'd developed so many improper eating habits over the years. I didn't regard food as medicine and nourishment, I viewed it as an activity and therapy. Food was my go-to for a reward or celebration, and it was also comfort if I was sad or nervous. I needed to be reprogrammed and started noticing how I'd reach for food or snacks out of habit even though I wasn't hungry.

> **I needed to be reprogrammed and started noticing how I'd reach for food or snacks out of habit even though I wasn't hungry.**

After the fast, and once I incorporated my new regimen, I was more aware of my actions, making it easier to break those bad habits. I read a lot of books about food and how the over consumption of bad foods can produce a lot of mucus in your body. Mucus prohibits your immune system from being able to combat diseases. This was a real eye-opener for me. Afterall, I **was** responsible for everything I consumed, and I couldn't confess to be happy, healthy, and whole yet consume foods that would bring about the opposite results of my confession.

Consequently, the lifestyle diet the Lord gave me aided in better sleep and more energy and my family noticed. Eventually, my husband and daughter made a few lifestyle changes as well. At one point, I was taking medicine for anxiety and clinical depression, but through the Lord educating me about the things that were contributing to it, I was able to completely stop taking medicine. I have a maintenance plan that I follow to the letter and it's been miraculous for my overall health.

The Word of God says the Holy Spirit will teach you all things (John 14:26) and that wisdom is freely given to those who ask (James 1:5). I leaned on the Holy Spirit for daily guidance and at times, hourly help, and I received it without fail. Wisdom is the application of knowledge. I was required to be a hearer and doer of the education I was receiving from the Holy Spirit in order to see results.

There were times when I'd deviate from my physical workout regime and lifestyle diet and within three weeks, I'd begin to feel and look bad. I noticed that my mental acuity would be affected as well then; my sleep patterns became inconsistent. The Lord said, "Stacey, all of this is connected. Your health pillar encompasses mental, physical, and social well-being. You can't separate them from each other."

I'm grateful for fasting and prayer because I get what the *New International Version* of Isaiah 58:8 says, then your light will break forth like the dawn, and your healing will come quickly. Light is also known as knowledge. I began receiving knowledge about my health that was tailored just for me and I was healed.

My **family/relationship pillar** by far, was the one I received the most revelation about. I detail a great portion of it in Lesson 1, but I'll speak about my children in this lesson.

I have a daughter and two sons. They, like all children, are complete joys and make the world go around! When I began this process of pillar building, I prayed that my relationship with the Lord would inspire my children to want to serve the Lord wholeheartedly as well. I wanted them to catch sight of the growth in my life that they'd in turn, contribute only to the Lord. In this season, I witnessed a lot of deficits in their lives specific to their spiritual training. I asked the Lord to correct what I'd done incorrectly and to help me better parent them as teens and young adults.

> **I asked the Lord to correct what I'd done incorrectly and to help me better parent them as teens and young adults.**

Through prayer, I was able to see how disconnected I was from them. I was led to locate the notes and videos from their baby dedication ceremonies and any prophecies I received about them. I transcribed and emailed them to myself. I printed them out for their reference as well. I started disclosing exactly what the Lord said about them as children and over a season, I began to change how I parented. The Holy Spirit would reveal areas to pray about even while I was sleeping. There were times I'd go to sleep heavy-hearted and/or looking for answers to a problem they presented, I'd pray and worship and when I woke up I'd have real time answers and know exactly what to do. I truly believe the Holy Spirit is the best third parent, He loves our children completely and intensely!

All three of them were uniquely created with different purposes. My prayer was to join forces with Rozelle to help them discover what they were. I didn't want them to be like me and truly discover their life's work in their forties.

Once again, humility was my first area of growth. I apologized to them a lot for how I took parenting matters into my own hands and never consulted the Lord first. I spent time and communicated with them often, and over time, they felt more comfortable hanging out with me. Like any relationship, it's ceaseless work to build and maintain. My faith was challenged each time I saw them make a decision that didn't align with God's word.

I had a choice; to worry or speak life. I learned to speak life. Speaking life tests your faith. The Lord said, "Can you rehearse what I said about them regardless to what you're seeing right now?" This was a test that I was determined to pass. One of the sentences in my confession for them reads; "I will not be ashamed nor walk in guilt over the mistakes I've made as a parent, or the mistakes they make as children. Because there exactly that, 'missed takes' that God will edit and use for our perfecting, and His glory."

...there exactly that, 'missed takes' that God will edit and use for our perfecting, and His glory."

The more comfortable they felt with me, the more they began trusting me and asked me to pray for them when they needed it. I often told them at the time, "I'm the coolest 45-year-old you all know!" They'd burst out laughing and say, "No you're not, you're the weirdest," then we'd all laugh out loud! God was drawing us closer together and my heart was glad. I love them with my whole heart, and nothing would make me more contented, than to know they love the Lord and live to serve Him.

I heard Myles Munroe say, "You can't take credit for being a good parent until your **grandchildren** live for the Lord, not your children." That's a powerful statement because it shows that your Godly parenting has taken root, and the fruit of it shows in the next generation. Only the Lord can assist you in raising the children He selected and placed in your care.

My **career/finances pillar** was a little different because it was the tallest one on my sketch. Rozelle, and I, as declared in Lesson 16, disagreed about finances for the first 15 years of our marriage. Since then, we've submitted to the plan the Lord gave us and our finances have continually flourished, and we worked **together** to manage them. We increased our savings and investments exponentially and because we remain faithful and humble, God continues to open doors for us to manage more.

In addition to this new way of managing, the Lord told me to re-read a book by Edwin Louis Cole title *Communication, Sex and Money.* (1987) Although I had this book for over 25 years and introduced it to so many people, it spoke volumes in this season. The Money section of the book points out how character and finances go hand in hand. Louis Cole admonishes that we shouldn't foster financial relationships with people who don't exhibit Godly character and expounds on ten spectacular points specific to investing. I urge you to add this book to your library.

Your job should supplement your life's work until its able to sustain you.

For those of you who haven't begun or are early in your career, I charge you with working on your life's work in tandem with your job. Your job should supplement your life's work until its able to sustain you. As a word of caution, debt is not your friend and it brings added stress you don't need as you're still growing at this critical time in your life. There's good debt and bad debt. Bad debt essentially means you're living outside of your means and you're undisciplined. Utilize the resources around you to educate yourself and don't be afraid to ask for help. I recommend you read, *No More Debt! God's Strategy for Debt Cancellation* (2001) by Creflo Dollar. It's an excellent resource.

Bad debt essentially means you're living outside of your means and you're undisciplined.

For those of you who are building your careers, I charge you to put the same time and effort into your life's work. I didn't leave my career upon discovering my life's work, I continued to maintain it as the Lord directed me. Many of my colleagues offer me wonderful opportunities to continue advancing my career but I know they'll distract me from my life's work, so I turn them down. Yet again, I listen to the Lord as He knows best. Instead, I work in the evenings and weekends on my life's work as my income and bonuses fund the projects I'm directed to complete. I exercised discipline and didn't stray from my strict household budget; I know any additional income we receive has a specific purpose.

For my readers who are still pursuing their education, you're in a stellar position! You're able to establish some parameters **now** that'll prevent you from wasting precious time. Seek the Lord and discover your life's work now and work diligently to complete it in tandem with your education. You may find the Lord leads you in a new direction altogether.

Just remember nothing is ever "wasted" (time, jobs, internships, etc.,) in the Lord's eyes, He'll use every opportunity to advance you toward what He has in store for you. Your number one priority is to surround yourself around those who'll "sharpen" you and hold you accountable to your goals. (Proverbs 27:17) Keep in mind, as discussed throughout this Volume, the Lord completely funds His vision for you, no job is capable of doing so.

In conclusion, I pray you draw an honest depiction of your table and begin to work with the Lord on your plan for strength, evenness, and stability because He knows best!

Find your favorite translation of 3 John 2:1 and recite it daily.

Let's pray:

Father, you said it's impossible to please you if we don't have faith in you (Hebrews 11:6). We know that faith without doing what you say, produces death. I understand that each pillar is equally important and requires work simultaneously. I also understand that I don't need anyone's help to start working on my table but the Holy Spirit. Lord, I want to completely fulfill the purpose you've given me, and it begins with a proper foundation. I believe that there's absolutely nothing you <u>can't</u> do. You resurrect dead things and bring life to them again. Help me Holy Spirit, to submit to fasting and prayer so I can clearly hear your voice. Fasting and prayer is where I receive specific instructions and discover my path to complete victory. I thank you that my spiritual life, health, family, relationships, career, and finance pillars are all strong and balanced. I decry the spirit of pride and welcome humility to build and strengthen my pillars. As you heal me you are lifted up and draw more souls to your kingdom through my living model. In Jesus's name, Amen.

Lesson 13

Your Basement Has All the Answers, Now Consult the Experts!

*M*entoring women is one of my passions. Over the years, I've had the pleasure of ministering to some outstanding women via small groups in my home. The Lord would always orchestrate these groups of 4-6 women and ironically, they'd have so many things in common. We'd work through activities together that focused on a specific area of work. One month, we centered on being intentional about the not-so-obvious signs that indicate something is impeding our spiritual growth.

We asked ourselves; what are the things in our lives that's causing us to miss opportunities for growth and promotion?

Prior to our orientation meeting, I was praying for them and was led to research home and commercial building foundations. I came across a YouTube video for a company that specialized in home foundation repair. Our foundations are the place where everything stems from or rests on. If it's compromised in any way, the tell-tell signs will show and indicate exactly where the issue lies.

In that 2.5-minute video, I saw so many correlations to the Word of God and how we're to be mindful of the things that physically show above ground that our foundations are damaged below ground (Luke 6:48-49). It also displayed that we're to be diligent about recognizing and repairing them swiftly to minimize further damage and increased costs.

In the video they referenced their foundation **experts** are:

- Trained to notice cracking in the basement walls or above doors and windows.
- Trained to locate doors and windows that stick or don't open and close properly.
- Proficient in geographical soil types that have heavier clay mixtures and/or higher moisture levels.
- Skilled in deciphering if an addition to your home is pulling on the existing structure and causing the foundation to shift.
- Competent in recognizing foundation wall bowing in the basement.
- Able to know the difference between wall bowing or ground settling.
- Masters in applying the proper repair system to bring the foundation back to its original state.

I shared the video with the group and asked the ladies to honestly identify what "cracks" they had in their spiritual foundations. I asked what was below the ground that was causing doors and windows to stick or not open at all.

> **I asked what was below the ground that was causing doors and windows to stick or not open at all.**

Doors and windows are often synonymous with growth, opportunities, and promotion.

I asked them to be candid about their spiritual growth. Were they truly growing or were there things that was stunting their growth? As they prayed for guidance, the Lord revealed areas they needed to focus on, and these weren't obvious things.

One person was directed to concentrate on finding new employment, but through this path, a lot was revealed about her lack of trust in God. She learned that she really didn't trust God because she'd been disappointed so many times by her family and those closest to her. As a result, she worked long hours to support herself and her family and never had much free time to devote to her children. Over time, the stress of a demanding job and working long hours took a toll on her health and she was forced to take medical leave.

Above the surface, her "cracks" were major health issues and fatigue, but the "basement" revealed it was a lack of trust in God, pain, anger, disappointment, and parenting struggles, etc.

We all supported one another in this group and challenged each other to face the spiritual foundational work. If it were ignored it would only make matters worse over time. Just as it's true of our homes and apartments, whatever maintenance items we ignore only gets worse and more costly over time.

Whatever the case, we declared; "Your basement has all the answers!" Our basements are not visible, and we rarely go down there to inspect the walls and the foundation. However, it's your responsibility to do so, and when you discover an issue, don't be prideful, call the **experts**.

In the video, it referenced that building an addition onto your home without properly checking the stability of the foundation can be detrimental. In comparison, we talked about "additions" to their lives that were pulling on them and causing their foundation to shift, such as unhealthy relationships, new jobs, unresolved family issues, and more personal responsibility.

After we identified these things, we wanted to make certain we applied the proper repair system just as the video suggested.

If the home foundation is settling or sinking, you need the pier system, which goes in the ground under the footings and will lift the foundation back up. The pier system has at least 4 piers that are strategically placed under the footings of the foundation. So, I asked the ladies what group of people do they consult that are strong enough to help them "lift their spiritual foundation" back up? I assured them, we're not made to carry burdens alone and the Lord will place people in your life to assist you when you're sinking. It's second nature to hide and/or isolate yourself when you're in need of help and that's the enemy's strategy most of us fall prey to...isolation.

The video references wall anchors and beam braces, both these repair systems can be done from inside of the house in the basement. These anchors and braces are attached to the wall or beam and are slowly tightened. Over time, it will repair the foundation back to its original state. This repair isn't a quick fix; it's slow, methodical and follows a consistent schedule.

I asked the ladies:

1	Who were their wall anchors or beam systems?
2	Who are the people in their inner circles?
3	Who are the ones that are strategically positioned and connected to them?
4	Who do they trust to patiently "tighten and straighten them up?"

I spelled out in Lesson 6, that you **need** people who will challenge you to be your absolute best. These people are like Nathan in the Bible. Nathan wasn't intimidated by King David and he addressed his sin and shortcomings in love. (2 Samuel 12: 6-12)

We all agreed that this was a good visual exercise because it highlighted how we're inclined to steal away and isolate ourselves when we're in trouble or when the storms come. Storms are not made to be weathered alone. I was reminded of the people in my life who've been the experts. They were skilled in the area I needed support in. It takes humility to ask the experts for help and this is where most of us suffer in silence.

Let's define what an expert is. According to Google, an expert is a person who has a comprehensive and authoritative knowledge of or skill in an area. Comprehensive denotes a wide-ranging scope of research and experience. In summation, experts have fruit and/or experience to reinforce their knowledge, making them very valuable.

Years ago, I read an article about marriage and the author said, "Be sure you keep couples who are winning with evidence, in your support group. You should never consult with a novice about marriage matters." He was right. I include in Lesson 3 how we go above and beyond the call of duty to research and find the best doctors, dentists, teachers, and schools **before** we invest time and money into them. Our marriages should be no different. The people we have in our support circles may change as our marriage grows, but they should always include skilled experts.

> **The people we have in our support circles may change as our marriage grows, but they should always include skilled experts.**

I'm often asked, "Well, how do you know who you can trust?" And my answer is always - prayer. You should never talk to <u>any</u> human being about your marriage more than you talk to the Creator of your marriage. Prayer is number one. Most of us fail in this area because we want a human connection when we're hurting and most times, we choose the wrong people.

Normally, when we're in pain, we retreat because we feel no one else is encountering what we are at the time. That's a complete lie and it comes straight from the enemy. In some cases, we do the opposite and cry out destructively to anyone who'll listen. Both outlets are not the best for you.

With the rise of social media sites, it has gotten worse because we feel the need to filter and photo-shop our lives. Most people are giving false representations of what's really going on in their marriages and homes. I know this because we're all human and human behavior hasn't changed, nor will it ever change. Human behavior is very much predictable. Marriages go through seasons and changes, just like anything else in life that's alive. Don't be fooled into believing no one else is being challenged or in pain at times. Trust me, they are! When you remain quiet and pray, the Lord will direct you to someone you can talk to. Sometimes, that person <u>may not</u> be someone you closely associate with.

You can be assured that it's the Lord leading you because of five factors:

1	They listen intently (encouraging).
2	They share a hardship they've endured (transparent).
3	They challenge you to do the right thing (maturity).
4	They assure you of their confidentiality and pray with you (connection).
5	They challenge and follow up with you (accountability).

These are the factors to look and listen for in an expert. Marital struggles can be extremely daunting at times, which is why prayer is essential. Prayer will help you eliminate the novices. Novices only make your struggles worse, and some will relish in your pain and never offer sustainable solutions.

I was blessed to learn more about the authority of experts when Rozelle and I were vacationing in Florence, Italy, and we decided to take a tour to see a winery. I love nature and was fascinated with ascertaining another process that's referenced in the Bible. In John 15:1-8, Jesus is speaking about being the true vine. After visiting this winery and taking notes on the process of wine production, the Lord revealed so many wonderful correlations about marriage to me.

The tour began with our guide showing us the vineyard and explaining the color changes it would undergo. It was mid-October and he said, "We're in post-harvest and the colors we'll see in the upcoming weeks are yellow, red and then brown. Each of those colors lets us know if the branch is healthy and will produce grapes again next year."

My mouth was hanging wide open. Wow, nature tells us exactly if a vine branch is healthy and producing, making it very evident what to preserve and what to eliminate.

Jesus said His Father is the vine dresser and if we're not producing, we'll be cut off. When we're not producing, we detract from the nutrients that healthy branches need from the soil to survive. In marriage, you must trust that those who have weathered some storms can guide you through the ones you're encountering. They can clearly see what "nutrients" you're missing.

The tour guide then led us down to the cellars where the wine was aging in huge vats and barrels. He explained the life cycle of grape production. He said, "it takes five years before healthy vines start producing good grapes, then between the years of 10-30 they have maximum production, but minimum quality, during years 30-40 they have maximum quality however they produce less. At year 40 plus, whatever it produces is beautiful and taste the best."

At year 40 plus, whatever it produces is beautiful and taste the best."

Again, I was floored as the Holy Spirit correlated this magnificent process to marriage.

He said, "We enter marriage expecting to see fruit right away. We won't. It takes five years before you're considered "good and healthy" and just like grapes, this process can last up to 10 years." After your first decade of marriage and working together, you should have healthy fruit and then you can concentrate on quality. This process shouldn't be rushed as well. Season after season, you have specific work to do to increase your quality as a couple. The goal is 30+ years when you have maximum quality and value! How much easier would the early years be in marriage, if we told ourselves to focus on the decades not the individual years? The experts will teach you this concept so be sure to consult them.

My daughter's Godmother told me on our 10th anniversary that, "marriage is like the stock market, after 10 years there are always gains." She was right. She said, "Stacey, you focus on the decades when you purchase stock and don't watch it daily, otherwise you'll give up because it fluctuates so much." She was an expert and had been married 30 years at the time. Her next statement was the most philosophical, she said, "if you research ANY ten-year period of the stock market, there are always gains."

"If you research ANY ten-year period of the stock market, there is always gains."

She was absolutely correct. I have done extensive research on the stock market and ten-year increments is where the gains are, no matter which ten-year span you select to investigate there are consistent gains. When you're going through your growth changes and need advice, look for the healthy couples who have "maximum quality" and those who give you "beautiful advice that taste the best." They're the ones who are winning and have been producing for a few decades.

Let's pray:

Lord, I'll invest in my marriage. I won't emphasize day to day issues, but season to season growth. I understand that marriage growth is not to be rushed and our foundation must be set and firm before we build on it. I'll consistently look for cracks, bowing, and foundation settling that needs repair. I'll depend on your guidance through prayer and contact the experts you lead me to. I won't be prideful because we're all human and encounter the same things. I need support and I'll ask for it. I won't allow the enemy to isolate, silence and deceive me into thinking I'm the only person having growing pains. I know that social media isn't the truth, but a filtered and photo-shopped version of small snippets of our lives, therefore, I won't compare myself to others. Time, seasons, and hard work produce a healthy, long-lasting, and strong marriage not a social media post. I'll do my due diligence and seek you for you are the Creator of marriage and the best consultant for **my** marriage. I'll concentrate on doing my personal best and conquering goals one decade at a time. Thank you, Jesus, for giving me peace. In your Holy and Matchless Name, Amen.

This lesson is dedicated to Dr. Paul and Monica Jill King, who enjoyed 47 years of marriage gains before her passing in 2018.

In Honor of my magnificent and incomparable parents:
Terry Allen & Joyce Vernice Prater

And they have defeated him by the blood of the Lamb and by
their testimony. And they did not love their lives
so much that they were afraid to die.
Revelation 12:11 NLT

www.ingramcontent.com/pod-product-compliance
Lightning Source LLC
Chambersburg PA
CBHW070446090426
42735CB00012B/2474